The Woman Who Can't Forget

The Extraordinary Story of Living with the
Most Remarkable Memory Known to Science

A Memoir

JILL PRICE

WITH BART DAVIS

FREE PRESS

New York   London   Toronto   Sydney

B
P945

*f*P

FREE PRESS
A Division of Simon & Schuster, Inc.
1230 Avenue of the Americas
New York, NY 10020

First Free Press hardcover edition May 2008

FREE PRESS and colophon are
trademarks of Simon & Schuster, Inc.

For information about special discounts for bulk purchases,
please contact Simon & Schuster Special Sales at
1-800-456-6798 or business@simonandschuster.com

Designed by Kyoko Watanabe

Manufactured in the United States of America

1   3   5   7   9   10   8   6   4   2

Library of Congress Cataloging-in-Publication Data

Price, Jill.
The woman who can't forget : the extraordinary story of living with the
most remarkable memory known to science / Jill Price with Bart Davis.
        p.   cm.
Includes bibliographical references (p.   ).
1. Price, Jill, 1965–.   2. Long-term memory—Biography.   3. Memory disorders—
Patients—California—Biography.   I. Davis, Bart, 1950–.   II. Title.
        BF378.L65P75   2008
        153.1'2092—dc22
        [B]   2008004257
        ISBN-13: 978-1-4165-6176-7
        ISBN-10:   1-4165-6176-5

This book is dedicated to the three people who
know me best and I love the most:
my mother Roz, my father Lenny, and my brother Michael

and

To my husband Jim, who made life beautiful and
bearable for me. I love and miss you.

. . . and Walter

CONTENTS

PROLOGUE

The memory is sometimes so retentive, so service-
able, so obedient; at others, so bewildered and so
weak; and at others again, so tyrannic, so beyond
control!
                —Fanny Price, in Jane Austen's *Mansfield Park*

I know very well how tyrannical the memory can be. I
have the first diagnosed case of a memory condition
that the scientists who have studied me termed hyperthymestic syndrome—the continuous, automatic autobiographical recall of every day of my life from when I was
age fourteen on. My memory started to become shock-
ingly complete in 1974, when I was eight years old. From
1980 on, it is near perfect. Give me a date from that year
forward and I can instantly tell you what day of the week
it was, what I did on that day, and any major event that
took place—or even minor events—as long as I heard
about them on that day.

My memories are like scenes from home movies of every day of my life, constantly playing in my head, flashing forward and backward through the years relentlessly, taking me to any given moment, entirely of their own volition. Imagine if someone had made videos of you from the time you were a child, following you around all day, day by day, and then combined them all onto one DVD, and you sat in a room and watched that DVD on a machine set to shuffle randomly through all the tracks. There you are as a ten-year-old in your family room watching *The Brady Bunch;* then you're whisked off to a scene of you at seventeen driving around town with your best friends; and before long you're on the beach during a family vacation when you were three. That's how I experience my memories. I never know what I might remember next, and my recall is so vivid and true to life that it's as though I'm actually reliving the days, for good and for bad.

I can recall memories at will when I'm asked to, but on a regular basis my remembering is automatic. I don't make any effort to call memories up; they just fill my mind. In fact, they're not under my conscious control, and much as I'd like to, I can't stop them. They will pop into my head, maybe triggered by someone mentioning a date or a name, or I'll hear a song on the radio, and whether I want to return to a particular time or not, my mind is off and running right to that moment. My recall doesn't stop there, with one memory; it rushes from one to a next and a next, flipping wildly through days as though they're cards in a Rolodex.

As I grew up and more and more memories were stored in my brain, more and more of them flashed through my mind in this endless barrage, and I became a prisoner to my memory. The emotional stress of the rush of memories was compounded by the fact that because my memory worked so differently from the norm, it was incredibly difficult to explain to anyone else what was going on in my mind. I had a condition that had never before been diagnosed, and as much as I would try to explain how my memories assaulted me, my parents couldn't really grasp the nature of what was happening.

My mother would tell me not to dwell on things so much, and I'd try to explain that I wasn't dwelling, that the memories just flooded my mind. But that didn't make any sense to her. Nobody could understand, including me, and in time I was so frustrated by trying to describe the experience that I simply gave up and began keeping it almost entirely to myself.

Though I hate the idea of losing any of my memories, it's also true that learning how to manage a life in the present with so much of the past continually replaying itself in my mind has been quite a challenge, often a debilitating one. I have struggled through many difficult episodes of being emotionally overwhelmed by my memory through the course of my life. Then finally I decided I had to reach out and try to discover whatever I could about what was going on in my head and why. By a stroke of what now seems to me divine providence, I went online and did a search for "memory," and to my great good fortune, the first entry that came up was to Dr. James McGaugh, a leading memory researcher affiliated with the University of California at Irvine (UCI).

I had been sure that my search would send me to some Web site all about memory and that I'd read about other people like me. Little did I know just how unusual my condition is. Though nothing on the Web could explain my memory, the next best thing it could have done was to take me to Dr. McGaugh. He is one of the foremost memory experts in the world and the author of over 500 scientific papers on human memory. His list of awards and honors was impressive, and I saw that he had lectured at a host of universities and institutions around the world. I can't say that I understood much of what I read about his work—the titles of the papers alone were daunting—but as soon as I found him, I thought, "This is the man who's going to tell me what's going on."

Even so, I felt some trepidation about contacting him. Would he be interested in me? Would he have time for me? I would be contacting him out of the blue, and he was clearly a very busy man. It took me three days to compose an e-mail to him, but at last, on June 8, 2000, I sent it off:

Dear Dr. McGaugh,

As I sit here trying to figure out where to begin explaining why I am writing you and your colleague, I just hope somehow you can help me. I am thirty-four years old and since I was eleven I have had this unbelievable ability to recall my past. I can take a date, between 1974 and today, and tell you what day it falls on, what I was doing that day and if anything of great importance occurred on that day. Whenever I see a date flash on the television I automatically go back to that day and remember where I was and what I was doing. It is non-stop, uncontrollable, and totally exhausting. . . .

Amazingly, he responded within 90 minutes, saying that if I lived anywhere close to UCI, he would be interested in meeting with me. That was a watershed moment in my life. How fortunate that I lived right up the highway from him, only an hour away in Los Angeles.

Though I was nervous and even scared about reaching out to the scientific community, the clarification and validation the scientists have given me about how my memory works, and that it is so unusual, has been a source of significant comfort. I am also greatly heartened to have learned that it turns out that the ways in which my memory is so different shed a good deal of light on many important mysteries about memory—and also about forgetting. My hope now is that the study of my memory will not only hold answers to long-standing questions about how normal human memory works but may lead to significant findings about the tragic disorders of memory loss.

The work I've done with Dr. McGaugh and his team has already helped me to see not only my own life in new terms, but also the lives of others and how memory plays such a powerful role in everyone's life. I've realized with more clarity, as I've reflected on my life in the process of writing this book and been exposed to findings in a broad range of memory science, just how profoundly our memories assist in constructing our sense of who we are and of the meaning of our lives. Whereas people generally create narratives of their lives that are fashioned by a process of selective remembering and an enormous amount of forgetting, and continually recraft that narrative through the course of life, I have not been able to do so. I came to realize in a flash of insight one day that whereas memory generally contributes to the construction of our sense of self, in my case, in so many ways my memory *is* my sense of self.

I do have a storehouse of memories that are more important to me than others and that I travel to often in my mind for comfort and as a refuge, but I have all the other days there too, impressing themselves on me all the time. It's as though I have all of my prior selves still inside me, the self I was on every day of my life, like her or not, nested as in a Russian doll—inside today's Jill are complete replicas of yesterday's Jill and the Jills for all the days stretching so far back in time. In that sense, I don't so much have a story of my self as I have a remarkably detailed memory of my self. Paring that down to cut out the mass of daily events and focus on the ways in which my memory has operated and has shaped my life has been a strange, sometimes mind-boggling experience, but one for which I am grateful because it has given me more clarity about the forces that have shaped my life.

I have always been a private person, and the decision to venture into the open about my memory was wrenching for me. But I've decided to tell the story of my journey because my work with the scientists has helped me to understand so much better that the way my memory works can throw useful light on what memory means in everyone's lives.

My greatest hope is that eventually scientists will discover something about my brain that will help solve the riddles of the tragic disorders of memory loss. The scientists have already determined from the scans of my brain that there are pronounced structural differences that probably account for why my memory is so complete and so relentless. I've learned from them how many mysteries about memory they're still grappling with, and it does seem that what they've learned about my brain and memory will lead to fruitful research. For now, I hope that my story is illuminating and thought provoking for readers; and helps explain the role of memory in all of our lives— as well as that of forgetting—and how our memories to such a significant degree make us who we are.

CHAPTER ONE

Alone with My Memory

You have to begin to lose your memory, if only in bits and pieces, to realize that memory makes our lives. Life without memory is no life at all. . . . Our memory is our coherence, our reason, our feeling, even our action. Without it, we are nothing.

—Luis Buñuel, *Memoirs*

Why is it that solitary confinement, without labor, is regarded as the severest form of imprisonment? It is because the lonely victim can find nothing to do but to remember. And this incessant remembering has often proved more than the mind could bear.

—Reverend D. B. Coe, *The Memory of the Lost*

Time has one fundamental principle: it moves forward. We go from birth to death, from first to last. We are young before we grow old, stimulus always precedes response, and there is no return to yesterday. The sole exception is memory. For me, because of the way my memory works, not only do I often return to yesterday, I can never escape it. I live with a constant, unstoppable parade of the yesterdays of my life flashing furiously through my mind.

Give me a date, and I will travel right to some particular moment of that day and tell you what I was doing, as well as what day of the week it was and any major event that happened that day, as long as I heard about it then, in addition to certain events that pop into my mind that happened around the same time. *November 14, 1981,* a Saturday: My dad's forty-fifth birthday. That night a school group I was joining, the Rasonians, was initiating new members and taking us out in Westwood. *July 18, 1984,* a Wednesday: A quiet summer day. I picked up the book *Helter Skelter* and read it for the second time. In ten days, Saturday, July 28, Los Angeles would be hosting the Summer Olympics. *February 14, 1998,* a Saturday: I was working as a researcher on a television special and went into work to pick clips, a job I loved because I'm a TV fanatic.

My recall also works the other way: if you ask me about an event, again from 1980 onward, as long as I heard about it, I can give you the date and day of the week it happened, and related information. *The end of the FBI siege on the Branch Davidian compound*: Monday, April 19, 1993. It began on Sunday, February 28, 1993, two days after the World Trade Center bombing on Friday, February 26, 1993. *The final episode of* MASH *airs:* Monday, February 28, 1983. It was raining that day and the next day when I was driving my car, the windshield wipers stopped working. *The nuclear reactor in Chernobyl melts down:* Saturday, April 26, 1986. I was visiting friends in Phoenix. *The day the Chinese army brutally suppressed protests in Tiananmen Square:* Sunday, June 4, 1989. My aunt Pauline had just passed away, so we were taking my grandmother, her sister, to lunch at Eddie Saul's Deli to break the news to her.

This ability to automatically recall not only dates but also days of the week for events, and then to flip that and recall events for dates, was the feature of my memory that initially startled Dr. McGaugh, because it was unique in the annals of memory research.

That first day I met him—Saturday, June 24, 2000— automatic recall was the kind of test that he gave me. I was excited driving down from Los Angeles to meet him at the research complex at UCI. Though I was desperately hoping that Dr. McGaugh would be able to tell me why my memory works the way it does, I was also a bit unnerved about what I might learn. Who knew what odd brain condition I might have? I had also kept so much to myself for so long about how insistent my memories were, and how they ruled my life, that the concept of disclosing to a complete stranger the weird phenomenon that was raging in my mind was disconcerting. I felt that

I'd be exposing my innermost self—a self that I had not even truly revealed to my family and friends because I hadn't known how to make them understand. But I just had to know, finally, what was going on in my head, and my excitement about Dr. McGaugh having agreed to meet with me far outweighed my trepidation.

As I walked up to the research building, there he was, waiting outside for me, and from the moment he greeted me, he put me at ease. First, he gave me a simple test, which was the beginning of a process of discovery that has changed my life in so many ways.

We went up to his lab, and he had a big reference book lying on the table we sat down at—*The 20th Century Day by Day*. He pulled two lists out of the book that he had prepared from it. One was of historically important events occurring during the past thirty years—roughly the period of my strong memory—and the other was a list of dates. He started with the list of dates and asked me to tell him what event had happened on each.

The first date on the list was November 5, 1979, and I immediately told him it was a Monday but that I didn't know what happened on that day. On the day before, though, on November 4 of that year, I said, the Iranian students had invaded the U.S. embassy in Tehran and taken the hostages whom they held for 444 days. He shook his head and said, no, that happened on the fifth. I told him I was sure it had happened on November 4, and because I was so adamant, he decided to check another source.

When it turned out that I was right and the book was wrong, I could see that Dr. McGaugh was stunned. I was right about all of the other dates on the list too. Then he quizzed me about the second list, which was of events, asking me to give him the date they happened. I got every one of those right too, and as Dr. McGaugh explained to me, one of the things that surprised him the most was how automatic my answers were. He was intrigued that I was clearly not actively trying to recall the answers; they were just there for immediate access. The complete lists, with the answers I gave, as they were reproduced in the paper Dr. McGaugh wrote about me years later, were as follows. Note that in the scientific paper, the scientists referred to me as AJ, in the tradition of preserving the anonymity of subjects of research:

ANSWERS (EVENTS) AJ GAVE TO DATES

DATE	EVENT
8/16/77	Tuesday, Elvis died
6/6/78	Tuesday, Proposition 13 passed in CA
5/25/79	Friday, Plane crash, Chicago
11/4/79	Sunday, Iranian invasion of US Embassy
5/18/80	Sunday, Mt. St Helens erupted
10/23/83	Wednesday, Bombing in Beirut, killed 300

1/17/94   Monday, Northridge Earthquake
12/21/88   Wednesday, Lockerby [Lockerbie] Plane
           Crash
5/3/91   Friday, Last Episode of *Dallas*
5/4/01   Friday, Robert Blake's Wife Killed

ANSWERS (DATES) AJ GAVE TO EVENTS

EVENT	DATE
San Diego Plane Crash	Monday, September 25, 1978
Who Shot JR?	Friday, November 21, 1980
Gulf War	Wednesday, January 16, 1991
Rodney King Beating	Sunday, March 3, 1991
OJ Simpson Verdict	Tuesday, October 3, 1995
Atlanta Bombing	Friday, July 26, 1996
Death of Princess Diana	Saturday/Sunday, August 30–31, 1997 (depending on France or US)
Concorde Crash	Tuesday, July 25, 2000
Election Dates:	
G. W. Bush	Tuesday, November 7, 2000
W. Clinton	Tuesday, Nov 3, 1992 and Tuesday, November 5, 1996

When I explained to him that I could also report my recollection of what I was doing personally on those

dates, he was intrigued and asked me to write those recollections down. I did so in about fifteen minutes. Some
of the events of those days I'd rather not refer to, and in
the paper and here as well, we just indicated that they
were personal:

Monday, September 25, 1978: It was my
grandmother's birthday and I had just started the
8th grade. The plane crash was a PSA flight over
San Diego. A member of our Temple was on that
flight.

Friday, November 21, 1980: I was in the 10th grade
and I went to the Homecoming football game at my
high school and then I went to Karen's house to
watch *Dallas.* That was also the day that the MGM
Grand Hotel went up in flames in Las Vegas.

Wednesday, January 16, 1991: I was watching Casper
[Caspar] Weinberger on CNN and they broke in
with the news that we were at war. I looked out the
window and wondered how people could go on with
life as usual when we were at war. I felt the same
way on Tuesday 1/28/1986 when the *Challenger*
exploded.

Sunday, March 3, 1991: Personal

Tuesday, October 3, 1995: Sitting in my den
watching and waiting

Friday, July 26, 1996: I was having dinner at the Daily Grill with my friend Andi and I saw a lot of people standing around the television in the bar area so I went over there to see what was going on. I could not believe it.

Sunday, August 30, 1997: My friend Robin and I went shopping at Macy's and then went to Hamburger Hamlet for dinner. After getting home, at 10 p.m., I put on *The Practice* on ABC and found out the princess had died.

Tuesday, July 25, 2000: I was working and read about the crash on the Internet.

Tuesday, November 7, 2000: Personal

Tuesday, Nov 3, 1992: My dad and I were so happy to vote for Clinton that I was dancing around the parking lot. We came home and my mom had bagels and lox for us to celebrate. That night I went over to my friend Stacy's house to watch his acceptance speech.

Tuesday, November 5, 1996: The family went to The Grill in Beverly Hills for dinner to celebrate [my brother] Michael's birthday which was the next day.

As you can see, the recollections I get for any given date tend to be snippets at first. When I'm given a date, I have an immediate recall of some particular thing, or a few things, that happened that day. My mind takes me right to those moments, and I in effect am "in" them again; I also feel the emotion of whatever moment has popped up. If I start to focus on recalling more, I'll "see" more and more of the day.

The fact that my memory is not only for dates and for cultural or news events but for those events combined with the events of my own life is the reason that Dr. Mc-Gaugh identified it as distinctively autobiographical in nature. Researchers distinguish among many types of memory, for example, short-term, long-term, semantic, episodic, and working memory. There are many more. Each has its own particular functioning, and scientists are still working out how the various types of memory are created and stored in the brain and how they combine with one another in day-to-day life. For example, they have theories about how short-term memories are transformed into long-term ones, but no definitive answer. Autobiographical memory is a combination of long-term memory for the specific events in our lives, such as, for me, going to Disneyland with a good friend of mine, and knowledge about the facts of our lives, such as that we are married or that we have two children. Most people's autobiographical memory is highly selective, emphasizing particularly important or emotionally intense events, such as one's wedding day or a horrible car accident.

What was so striking to Dr. McGaugh about that first

test he did of my memory is that in the study of what is called superior memory, my type of autobiographical recall was unheard of. That's why the scientists coined a new term for it: hyperthymestic syndrome, from the Greek words *thymesis,* which means remembering, and *hyper,* meaning extreme or excessive. One of my hopes is that people who have been living with the syndrome will hear word of it, as I know all too well how confusing and difficult it is to cope with and what a comfort it has been to me to understand the condition better—even just to know that I have a specific condition.

What is so different about my sort of recall is that most cases of superior memory involve the ability to remember other types of information, such as strings of numbers like the digits of pi or long lists of unrelated words. My memory doesn't work that way at all, and I did not perform especially well on tests that measure that sort of memorization ability. The previously documented cases of superior memory break down into two main types: people who use mnemonic devices such as imagery or rhyming to memorize vast amounts of data and savants who are naturally able to memorize incredible volumes of information, like the entire New York City phone book or a hundred years of baseball statistics. I can't even imagine doing that.

The history of methods for memorizing is fascinating, stretching all the way back to ancient times. One technique, called the method of loci, is attributed to the

Greek poet Simonedes of Kos in 447 B.C. It consists of mentally walking down a familiar path and attaching to-be-remembered facts to places along the path. When you want to recall them, you "walk" along the path in your mind, and they are much more easily retrieved. I've never used mnemonic tricks like this or rehearsed the events of my life in order to remember them. Nor do I use any kind of memory aids like rhyming or imaging items in my head. I'm as awed by the feats of that sort of memorizing as anyone else is.

One of the most famous cases of superior memory is of a man referred to in the scientific literature as S, who was studied by Russian psychologist Alexander Luria. Luria's attention was brought to S, whose name was later revealed to be Solomon Veniaminovich Shereshevskii, by the editor of the newspaper where S worked. The editor had noted that after the morning meeting he held with the reporters, S was able to recall lengthy instructions he'd been given without having taken any notes. Luria tested S at length and concluded that his memory was phenomenally strong, and that although he used some mnemonic devices, his memory was not dependent on them. More recent scrutiny of Luria's work on S suggests that mnemonics might have been more integral to S's ability. Regardless of whether they were necessary for his remembering, he certainly was good at using them, as he later went on to become a professional mnemonist, performing memory feats for entertainment.

Interestingly, as is often the case with unusual types of memory, S also demonstrated other oddities in his mental abilities. He had a condition known as synesthesia, in which when one of the senses is aroused, it produces an associated sensation in another of the senses. When the person hears a certain sound, he might also see a color associated with it, or a taste might trigger an associated sound. S also had trouble with language: he couldn't understand that two different words could be used to refer to the same thing and could not comprehend abstract concepts. In addition, he had limitations with some types of visual recognition; when shown two pictures of the same person's face, he had trouble understanding that they were of the same face if the expressions were different. As is so often the case in the study of people with unusual memory abilities, these other quirks in S's mental functioning offered rich clues for investigation of the ways in which memory is so intricately intertwined with other thought processes in our brains. To me, the most interesting aspect of his story is that he had no superior memory for his own life events. The details about his own life were something of a blur.

There was also no evidence of superior autobiographical memory in another of the famous cases of superior memory, that of VP, a man who could play up to sixty games of correspondence chess without notes. By the age of five, he had memorized the street map of Riga, in Latvia, his home town of 500,000 people.

VP was able to memorize almost all of "The War of the Ghosts," a strange Native American folk tale that pioneering British psychologist Sir Frederic Charles Bartlett used to test people's memories because it is so quirky and hard to recall. He recited the story to those he was testing and then would ask them to recall it verbally to him. Most people leave out key details and change the story in significant ways. Here it is, in case you want to read it and test yourself about how much you can remember (though I warn you, it's odd):

One night two young men from Egulac went down to the river to hunt seals and while they were there it became foggy and calm. Then they heard warcries, and they thought: "Maybe this is a war-party." They escaped to the shore, and hid behind a log. Now canoes came up, and they heard the noise of paddles, and saw one canoe coming up to them. There were five men in the canoe, and they said:

"What do you think? We wish to take you along. We are going up the river to make war on the people."

One of the young men said, "I have no arrows."

"Arrows are in the canoe," they said.

"I will not go along. I might be killed. My relatives do not know where I have gone. But you," he said, turning to the other, "may go with them."

So one of the young men went, but the other returned home.

And the warriors went on up the river to a town on the other side of Kalama. The people came down to the water and they began to fight, and many were killed. But presently the young man heard one of the warriors say, "Quick, let us go home: that Indian has been hit." Now he thought: "Oh, they are ghosts." He did not feel sick, but they said he had been shot.

So the canoes went back to Egulac and the young man went ashore to his house and made a fire. And he told everybody and said: "Behold I accompanied the ghosts, and we went to fight. Many of our fellows were killed, and many of those who attacked us were killed. They said I was hit, and I did not feel sick."

He told it all, and then he became quiet. When the sun rose he fell down. Something black came out of his mouth. His face became contorted. The people jumped up and cried.

He was dead.

VP was able to recall the story with remarkable precision six weeks after listening to only two readings of it. A year later, he was able to recall the tale just as accurately as he had the year before.

When I was asked to read the story and recall it, I just said, "No way," because I knew from experience that I wasn't going to be able to remember it. That's not the way my memory works. I did finally agree to read it, and recalled only seven out of forty-nine nouns and eight out of sixty-eight verbs. By contrast, VP's score was thirty-three out of forty-nine nouns and forty out of sixty-eight verbs, and his score was almost as high six weeks later.

Another test I was given in order to compare my memory to cases like that of S and VP was about number recall. I was asked to look at a 4 × 13 matrix of numbers, such as this below, and recall as much of it as I could right thereafter:

6	6	8	0
5	4	3	2
1	6	8	4
7	9	3	5
4	2	3	7
3	8	9	1
1	0	0	2
3	4	6	1
2	7	6	8
1	9	2	6
2	9	6	7
5	5	2	0
x	0	1	x

S was able to call off all fifty-two numbers in succession in 40 seconds after studying the matrix for only three minutes. I just laughed when they asked me to do this test. Were they kidding? I studied the matrix for 3 minutes 52 seconds and was able to recall only seven of the fifty-two numbers.

In one book about studies of people with unusual memory, out of ten cases described, the majority had an incredible memory only for quite specific kinds of information, which they had memorized. For example, subject A had worked as a telephone operator in Britain and was able to recall nearly all the telephone exchange codes of all the towns in the British Isles. None of the ten cases, however, had more than average ability to recall autobiographical detail from their pasts. Clearly my brain works quite differently from theirs.

As for savants such as Kim Peek, the inspiration for the character in the movie *Rain Man,* they tend to have particular areas of extraordinary memory, such as the ability to remember long displays of words or digits, but they do not generally have extraordinary autobiographical recall. I am neither autistic nor a savant, and the kind of calculations they do with strings of thousands of words or numbers are as foreign to me as they are to you.

In fact, I'm horrible at memorizing. Many people have commented that school must have been a breeze for me. But my memory was actually more of a hindrance than a help in school. My mind doesn't store information in the way that so much of school requires. I had lots of trouble memorizing history, arithmetic, foreign language, and science facts because I had to be genuinely interested in information of that kind in order to remember it. Memorizing poetry was especially painful, if not impossible. I needed math tutors from second grade on to help me memorize the way to do calculations, and I did horribly in geometry because I could never remember the theorems. Not only is my brain not good at that type of remembering, but over time, the constant rush of personal memories running through my head made it hard to pay attention. The result was my grades were mostly Cs with some Bs and an A here and there. This is also one reason that the fact that I had a superior memory didn't become clear to my parents and teachers as I was growing up.

Though this may sound odd, the fact that my memory is so different wasn't always clear even to me. When I was young, I had a vague sense that I seemed to have a much better memory than lots of other people. I was always correcting my parents about things they claimed I had said, or that they had said to me, which, as you can imagine, didn't go over very well. But my memory wasn't always so strikingly different; it seems to have developed in stages as I grew up, and up to my mid-elementary school years, it wasn't something that preoccupied me.

I first began to appreciate just how detailed my memory was becoming in 1978, at age twelve. I was in seventh grade and studying on May 30 for a science final with my mother. That was a bad year at school, and as I studied, I started to drift off into thinking how much I had loved the year before. Suddenly I was aware that I was able to vividly recall exactly what I was doing the same day the year before. May 30 that year was Memorial Day, and I saw myself on Tees Beach in Santa Monica with my family by lifeguard station 4. I had another such vivid memory a couple of months later, on July 1. I was on the beach at Paradise Cove with my friend Kathy and her family, and she and I were eating vanilla custards. All of a sudden I realized that she and I had done exactly the same thing on the same beach on the same day the year before. I looked at her and said, "Do you realize we did the exact same thing on July 1 last year?" expecting that shock of recognition when she too remembered the day. But she just looked at me and said, "We did?" and I realized she didn't remember it at all. That was when I started to understand that my memory was unusual, and from then on, flashes of recall of that kind just kept happening more and more.

I can clearly identify three phases of my memory's development. For my earliest years, from 1965, when I was born, to 1974, I remember a good deal more than most other people do from that part of their lives. I also have some vivid memories from much younger than the age of most people's first memories. My earliest memory is from when I was eighteen months old and I was in my crib. My uncle's poodle, Frenchie, woke me up, and when I opened my eyes, there he was, his big brown eyes staring at me in curiosity, and I started crying. (Before long, I grew to love Frenchie.)

From 1974 to 1979, ages eight to thirteen, I remember most days but not every day, and I sometimes have to try for a few seconds to recall a day. From February 5,

1980, onward is when I begin to have completely accurate recall.

My memory for dates and days of the week seems to have evolved naturally right along with my recall of events as I grew up. One of the results was that I began to simply "see" in my mind that certain years matched up by date. For example, 1969 and 1986 have exactly the same calendars, meaning that all the dates fell on the same days. January 1 was a Wednesday in both years, and all of the rest of the days were the same through the year.

My memory is constantly making linkages between dates that way. For example, I often do what I call "chaining" through these identical years. From a given date that has popped into my mind—say, July 4, 2007, which fell on a Wednesday—I'll find my memory drawn to traveling back to all of the other July 4ths in my life, from the period of my strong recall, that also fell on a Wednesday: in 1990, 1984, and 1979. I do this not only for days in years with identical calendars, though; I like doing it for any given date, chaining quickly back through all the days with the same date and seeing what nugget of memory first pops up for each day. This is soothing for me, bringing some order to the swirl of my memories, and often when I'm blow-drying my hair in the morning, I flip through all the days with the same date as that morning. The other day, December 19, for example, I wrote up a description of my recall as I chained through all of the

December 19ths that I can remember, starting in 1980.
I'll spare you the complete write-up, as I'm sure a selection will make the point:

DECEMBER 19, 1980—FRIDAY
Last day of school (10th grade) before Christmas
vacation.

That night babysit for the Reisberg sisters
(5 and 7).

DECEMBER 19, 1981—SATURDAY
Go shopping with Dean and Harry in Beverly
Hills. See Candace in Beverly Hills—she just made
the cheerleading one day earlier and she was so
happy!

That night go out with Harry—I am wearing
my gray turtleneck sweater and I break my
bracelet on his bed; we go to Swenson's Ice
Cream.

DECEMBER 19, 1982—SUNDAY
My third day as a box girl at Gelson's supermarket.

That night I went to see *Six Weeks* with Dudley
Moore and Mary Tyler Moore; it was so sad and we
were all crying. Liz slipped on wet paper on the
floor and slid across the theater lobby.

DECEMBER 19, 1983—MONDAY
Home from college for Christmas vacation. My
first (and last) day as a flower deliverer at the

flower shop across the street from Renee's mom's
shop. Get locked in an elevator. Get chased by a
squirrel at The Buckley School. Get lost in Sun
Valley. Get pulled over on the 405 south for
tailgating on my way to Westwood to see *Silkwood*.
I was with Renee, Susie and Tricia.

DECEMBER 19, 1984—WEDNESDAY (LEAP YEAR)
Finish first semester at LAVC (community college).
Candace over and we watch *Charles in Charge*. We are
really excited because we are going to AZ in the
morning.

DECEMBER 19, 1985—THURSDAY
Finishing up Fall 85 semester at LAVC. I got my
hair cut really short the day before so now I had
really high hair and used a lot of Aqua Net Super
Hold. Michael [my brother] opened the door while
I was getting dressed and I slammed it shut but it
swung open into my eye. I was leaving for Florida
on my first trip without my parents (Boca to see
grandparents and aunt and uncle and Philadelphia
to see Cathi and Dan) on Sunday 12/22 and I had
a black eye.

DECEMBER 19, 1986—FRIDAY
Finishing up my time at LAVC.
Went to work at Nordstrom's Rack—HATED
THAT JOB.

Perhaps one reason that I remember days so well is that my brain seems to love to organize time. One of the unusual ways it does so, which intrigued the scientists because again it was so unprecedented, is with visuals that I just "see" in my mind. The first of these is a time line of history, which covers not just my lifetime but goes back to the year 1900. I have no idea why this is the case, nor do the scientists. The way I drew this time line for them is as follows:

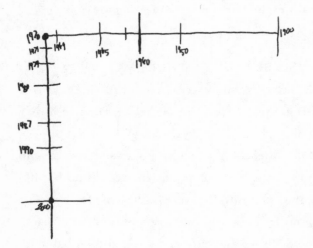

When they asked me to describe how I saw the time line on several different occasions, I always drew it exactly the same way, with the same set of years and with all of the lines the same range of lengths. I can't think of any reason that it's this particular set of years I see or why I draw some of the lines longer and some shorter. I also have no idea why 1970 is the pivot point at the top left, where the time line switches from horizontal to vertical.

The scientists remarked how counterintuitive it is that the dates start at the right and proceed to the left, like reading Hebrew, and then down rather than up. But to me that's not counterintuitive at all; it's simply the way I see them. They don't know what the significance of this time line is in the way my memory works or why I see history in this fashion. As far as I'm concerned, I can't imagine not seeing the time line in my mind.

That isn't the only visual that took shape in my mind as I grew up. I see single years as circles, as in the diagram below. June is always at the bottom and December always at the top, and the months progress counterclockwise.

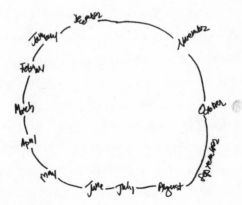

Because my memory became so complete, I began to act as the historian in my family and among my friends, regularly reminding people of the dates of events in their lives and "refereeing" disputes about when something happened. "No, it wasn't in July of 1998 that you two went to Italy, that was August of 1996." "You're both wrong. The date you had that huge fight was Saturday, November 16, 2002, and you patched it up on December 11." "Grandma didn't come to visit us in January that year; she came on March 14." I like dating events that way and don't mind at all when people ask me to do so. That's probably the most clarifying way in which people start to understand just how different my memory is. I even used to joke that I should open a "Stump the Human Calendar" booth on Venice Beach, near where I grew up in Los Angeles.

The truth is, though, that as much as I like that my memory is so complete, it's been terribly difficult to live with. My lack of talent for memorizing is only one of the many features of my memory that have influenced my life in ways that have been seriously challenging, often excruciating. One of the most troubling features of my memory is that it is so automatic and can spin wildly out of control. Though I can direct my memory back to particular events I want to remember—and when asked to, I can recall memories in a systematic way, such as when I'm given a date or an event—when my memory is left to its own devices, it roams through the course of my life at will. Memories are popping into my head randomly all the time, as though there is a screen in my head playing scenes from movies of years of my life that have been spliced into one another, hopping around from day to day, year to year, the good, the bad, the joyful, and the devastating, without my conscious control.

Perhaps they're not actually random. They do seem to be sparked by what scientists of memory call retrieval cues, such as a date being mentioned, a song on the radio, or a name coming up. The other day, for example, the song "Jessie's Girl" came on the radio, and instantly my memory went to the first day I heard the song, March 7, 1981. I had just gotten my driver's permit and I was driving my friend Ronni home after she spent the night at my house. Often it's a smell that will take me back. For example, when I walked into the house the other night, the first thing I smelled was a baked potato in the oven, and it brought me right back to when I was two years old, sitting in the living room in our apartment in New York City and watching Walter Cronkite on the *CBS Evening News*. For forty years that is exactly the moment that the smell of a baked potato always takes me back to. It's not the same if a potato is microwaved; the memory isn't triggered. It has to be baked in the oven.

Sometimes I'm aware of what the cue was, as in those cases, but many times I'm not. My recall is so automatic that I'm not truly conscious most times about why I have started remembering something.

According to one of the leading theories, normal human memory makes use of retrieval cues in this way too, probably because those words or sounds or smells were stored in the long-term memory at the same time the memory was. The more specific the cue is, the more effectively it tends to call up a memory. For example, if you went on a great trip to Yosemite Park, you might not find yourself remembering that trip if a friend just said the word *park*, but if she said *Yosemite*, the chances that your mind would flash onto that trip increase. I'm sure you can remember instances of a memory popping into your head that way when you heard a song or a place name. They're called involuntary memories, and one study showed that most people have about three to five of them a day. Ironically the memory of having these memories fades quickly for most people, so you may be able to recount only a couple of particular instances.

One of the things that seems to be different about my memory is that many things act powerfully and automatically as retrieval cues for me, filling my head with involuntary memories almost all the time. When I'm watching TV, I may hear a product name that will set off a rush of memories; or driving to work, I may notice a place name on a road sign, and my mind will take off. I have many, many more than three to five memories a day; they pop into my mind continually. Another key difference in my involuntary memories seems to be that normally, most such memories are of positive experiences, but mine are all over the map, from great times to horrible ones.

A key question about my memory, in fact, is whether I remember so much because so many of my long-term memories get stored with such a richness of cues. It may be that we all encode into our long-term memories as much information about our lives as I do, but that my mind has a much greater ability to pull those memories out of storage. The problem with how many cues set my memory off is that the process is constant, and my mind doesn't just flash on to those memories and then quickly get back to the present moment.

In many ways, my memory has been both a blessing and a curse. When I'm feeling down, I often revisit favorite memories, which I call "traveling," going back especially to the happiest years of my life as a young child in New York City and suburban New Jersey. I wouldn't give my memories of those years up for anything in the world; they give me great comfort during my most difficult times. But my memory has also caused me quite a bit of pain through the years. Remembering so many of the moments of my life means I recall not only the joyful, fun times: the times of wonderful family closeness and friendship and sharing, and the esteem-building moments of achievement. I also constantly recall the fights and the insults, the excruciating embarrassments, the moments of heated anger and devastating disappointment.

One of the features of my memories that is most difficult to cope with is that the emotion of them isn't dialed
down; my memories are apparently exceptionally emotional and sensually vivid. Some fascinating research has
been done on the question of how much emotion is recalled in normal human remembering. Most people—82
percent according to one study—report that they vividly
recall emotions along with their memories. But research
has shown that that is probably true for only a small set of
particularly momentous memories in their lives, which
are called personal event memories, and are experienced
as being relived when they are remembered.

Some studies have even indicated that for many memories that people report as being highly emotional, the
degree of emotion they experience while remembering
them is in fact quite faint. For example, when people
were asked to remember while their brains were being
scanned in real time, no activity in the emotional center
of the brain, the amygdala, was detected. An interesting
exercise to try in order to figure out what is true of your
own emotional recall, suggested to me by one researcher
who has worked on this question, is to quickly describe
twenty highly emotional memories. Apparently in the
studies she has done, this exercise is quite difficult for
most people after the first few items. But I could list hun-
dreds of them without stopping to think.

When I remember, the effect for all of my memories
is like that described for personal event memories. It's

not as though I'm looking back on the events with the distance of time and of adult perspective; it's as though I'm actually living through them again. Though it's difficult to describe this, when I remember, I see and feel with the fullness of watching a scene in a movie, and that can be emotionally overwhelming. For me, the emotion that comes along with every memory is every bit as potent as it was the day I first had it.

I feel the same fear, no matter how irrational that fear might have been. When we moved to Los Angeles in the summer of 1974, my parents were young and had a lot of friends and they would go out every weekend. Depending on what night of the weekend it was, we had either our housekeeper or a babysitter stay with my brother and me. The Friday night TV lineup on NBC that fall was *The Rockford Files* at 9 P.M. and *Police Woman* at 10 P.M. I always hoped my parents would be home when *The Rockford Files* ended at 10:00, even though I knew it would be hours before they would actually get back. As the closing credits ran and the theme song played, I would begin feeling anxious. I would have trouble getting to sleep afterward and would wake up in the middle of the night, usually around 2 A.M. If I saw that my parents' car was not in the carport, I would start to feel really sick inside. I would go and get their pictures and lie in bed holding them, so when they came home they always found me sleeping with a bunch of pictures clenched tightly. Until now they never knew the reason for finding me like that. I loved the show but, even now that I'm forty-two years old, *The Rockford Files* theme song gives me a knot in my stomach every time I hear it, bringing me right back to being eight years old.

At any given moment, anything at all that someone said to me, or some hurtful or ridiculous thing that I said to someone that I desperately wish I could take back, may pop into my mind and yank me back to that difficult day and exactly how I was feeling about myself. Often it's excruciating to relive the past this way. I know that people generally forget—eventually, anyway—most of the details of arguments they've had, or of hurtful things friends and family have said or done to them, and that they've said and done to others. Those memories might be called to mind if they have a similar experience that brings them forth, but generally, they are not floating constantly in and out of people's consciousness. Unfortunately, I regularly remember a vast storehouse of them, and vividly, from the time I was fourteen.

The emotional intensity of my memories, combined with the random nature in which they're always flashing through my mind, has, on and off through the course of my life, nearly driven me mad. As I grew older and more and more memories accumulated in my mind, my memory became not only a horrible distraction in trying to live my life today, but also the cause of my terrible struggle to come to terms with my feelings about my past. The more memories were stored, the harder and harder it became to cope with the rush of recalled events. So many painful memories kept asserting themselves. The thousands of things my parents said to discipline me, for example, or blurted out when they were having a bad day or when I provoked them have never faded.

Dr. McGaugh told me that first day I met with him that lots of people had contacted him through the years. He had stacks of e-mails from people saying that they had special memory abilities, but almost all had turned out not to truly have the capabilities they'd described. He was convinced that my abilities, though, were real, and I felt joy and relief when he said that he wanted to work with me. I had no idea what to expect about what he would discover, but I felt sure that at last I was going to be able to begin to understand my memory and explain it to those in my life in a way I'd never been able to do.

One of the interesting things Dr. McGaugh has explained to me during the course of our subsequent work together is that science knows a good deal about forms of impaired memory such as amnesia, but it knows very little about forms of superior memory. That was one reason he was so interested in studying my memory further. Not only did my memory appear to be unique, but in the science of memory, there is a long tradition of discoveries arising from the study of people with unusual types of memory.

As far back as 1885, psychologist Hermann Ebbinghaus wrote in his classic *Memory: A Contribution to Experi-*

mental Psychology that "our information comes almost exclusively from the observation of extreme and especially striking cases." I was to discover that my memory does in fact shed light on many of the fascinating questions about how our memories work and how they shape our lives. One of the most intriguing of those, and a first order of business in trying to understand the workings of my memory, is *why* I don't forget. As it turns out, forgetting is a topic of unexpectedly intriguing dimensions.

CHAPTER TWO

The Gift of Forgetting

There is a goddess of Memory, Mnemosyne; but none of Forgetting. Yet there should be, as they are twin sisters, twin powers, and walk on either side of us, disputing for sovereignty over us and who we are.
— Richard Holmes, *A Meander Through Memory and Forgetting*

Selection is the very keel on which our mental ship is built. And in this case of memory its utility is obvious. If we remembered everything, we should on most occasions be as ill off as if we remembered nothing.
— William James, *The Principles of Psychology*

I recently read a fascinating article by the famous neurologist Oliver Sacks about a man who has the opposite condition of mine: he remembers virtually nothing, suffering from a severe form of amnesia. He cannot even remember what he has been doing from one moment to the next. He does have some vestige of semantic memory—the recall about general knowledge—which allows him to remember who his wife is and that he loves her, but if she leaves the living room while they're watching TV to go into the kitchen and get a drink, when she comes back, he greets her as if she has been long gone and he is overjoyed to see her again. With other people, he has no ability to recall who they are at all. When I read about him, I thought to myself that as problematic as my memory has been to live with, I wouldn't trade it in, because it has made me who I am. I do wish, though, that some of my memories would dissolve away into the mists of inaccessible time. Though people tend to think of forgetting as an affliction and are disturbed by the loss of so much memory as they age, I've come to understand that there is a real value to being able to forget a good deal about our lives.

As often as I've realized that other people don't recall anywhere near as much detail about their lives as I do, I still find it hard to imagine doing all of that forgetting. Whenever people ask me to recall something for them—like the month they first met or when they moved into a new apartment—I find myself amazed that they've forgotten those things. I frankly can't imagine life when so much of what you've done and thought and felt has simply vanished. The other morning I was watching *Regis and Kelly*, and the guest was Alyssa Milano. They asked her what it was like to be acting in *Who's the Boss* when she was so young, because she started making the show when she was just eleven. She said, "It's funny; I watch some of these episodes and I cannot remember anything about filming them." I thought to myself that if I had that kind of what I call "vacant space" in my head, I would be horrified.

It seems sad to me that many people forget so much of their lives, especially the most special times. I was talking to a friend not long ago about what we were doing around Christmas 1985, and the fact that she did not remember every day of that December, or at least some of it, was shocking to me because that was when she met her first love, and so it was such a wonderful time for her. I asked the same friend the other day, "Do you remember when we went to Disneyland?" She had no recollection *at all* of even having gone on the trip, which astounded me. I told her right away that we went on Saturday, October 19, 1991, three days after a mass murder in Killion, Texas. Even after I had reminded her, she couldn't recall the trip. To me, that kind of forgetting is simply mind-boggling, and I can't see the value of it at all. But that said, normal forgetting of some kind does seem to play many helpful roles in our lives, and I'm sure being able to forget in some of the ways most people do would have done me a world of good.

One of the things that's fascinating to me about memory research is that the question of why we forget so much is still such an open one. The process of forgetting, it turns out, seems to be almost as mysterious as the process of remembering. Scientists aren't sure if normal forgetting is the result of so many moments not being stored securely in long-term memory, or if they are in fact stored away but we don't generally have access to them. One notion is that a much richer trove of memories is stored than most people are able to remember, but they degenerate physically over time. Others argue that the forgetting process is an active and purposeful one. Are our brains repressing memories of a good deal of our personal experience, perhaps because those times were painful or undermining of our self-esteem, or of a view of ourselves that is important to us? That's one theory. Another says that the key is that new information simply comes along and "interferes" with the old; we have mechanisms in our brains that specifically inhibit unnecessary or distracting memories.

Given how distracting my rush of memories is to me, the value of that process of memory inhibition is perfectly clear. What I find especially intriguing, though, about the description of that process is that my memory apparently operates so differently from the norm. The concept is that over time, we have many memories of such similar, mundane, repetitive life events of no particular consequence that this "clutter" blocks our memory of any given one of them. This is one of the things that my mind doesn't seem to do in the same way. I remember all of the clutter.

Dr. McGaugh told me that one of the unusual features of my memory, which the scientists were especially intrigued by, is just this—how comprehensive it is. It doesn't differentiate between the most dramatic or consequential events in my life, the somewhat significant benchmarks, and the completely banal day-to-day things. I remember the date my first boyfriend broke up with me—December 29, 1981—and more in the benchmark category, the date I started eighth grade—September 6, 1978, and that we started school a week early that year and ended a week late because we had a full month off for Christmas vacation. But I also remember that on Friday afternoon, October 19, 1979, I came home from school and had some soup because it was unusually cold that day. I know that my senior prom was on June 3, 1983, but I also remember that on Sunday, March 28, 1999, when my mother and I went to breakfast at the Encino Glen coffee shop, I ordered scrambled eggs and I had a headache.

My memory also extends to lots of things that didn't directly involve me but that I read about or heard about on TV or radio, some of which I found of great interest and others that were of no particular importance to me. Many people have vivid memories of a few especially dramatic news or popular culture events, such as hearing when John F. Kennedy and then Martin Luther King, Jr., were shot, or when the *Challenger* space shuttle exploded, which are often referred to as flashbulb memories. This sort of memory is formed about an event that was especially emotionally powerful, and they are not only about news events but also intense personal experiences, such as of being mugged or in a bad car accident. What's different for me is I don't have to feel any great degree of emotion in order to remember any particular thing, whether something from my own life or something I heard on the news. For example, I know that Bing Crosby died on a golf course in Spain on Friday, October 14, 1977, and though I was a fan of his movies, that news certainly wasn't traumatic for me. I heard about it when I was driving to soccer practice with my mom, just as we were turning into the parking lot at Balboa Park.

One of the types of daily information that I recall vividly that often amazes people is the episodes of TV shows I watched. I was a big fan of *All in the Family* while I was growing up, for example, and if you throw out a date during its original broadcast, when I watched it religiously, I can tell you which episode ran. *January 5, 1974,* a Saturday: Gloria and Mike are alone for the evening, and when Gloria makes the first move, it upsets Mike. He then makes up a girlfriend named Felicia. *September 22, 1976,* a Wednesday: Archie has an affair with a waitress. *October 16, 1977,* a Sunday: It is Edith's fiftieth birthday, and she is held at gunpoint by a rapist.

Truth be told, I hate the notion of forgetting. I'm happy that I can remember so many episodes of so many

46

TV shows I've loved through the years; that I can revisit any given day that I may suddenly think about and know what really happened to me that day; and that I know what people really said to me, and I to them, and exactly when. The accuracy of my recall is important to me, and the idea of losing some of my memories, or my recall of dates and days of the week, is actually anxiety provoking.

If it's true, though, that the normal memory has a talent for forgetting a host of happenings that we would otherwise find self-limiting or undermining, because they hold up a mirror to us about aspects of our lives and ourselves that we don't like, I do have to say that it would be a good thing for me if my mind had that talent. Imagine being able to remember every fight you ever had with a friend; every time someone let you down; all the stupid mistakes you've ever made; the meanest, most harmful things you've ever said to people and those they've said to you. Then imagine not being able to push them out of your mind no matter what you tried.

According to some recent research, the ability to push unwanted memories out of the mind seems to operate according to the same brain mechanism that empowers us to restrain ourselves physically, like stopping ourselves from slapping someone or from reaching for that extra piece of cake. Though I may not truly envy the ability to forget, this is a talent I can say without hesitation that I wish I had. Research shows that such "motivated forgetting," as it's called, not only works in the short term but does assist people in forgetting unwanted memories for the long haul.

Forgetting is clearly of many kinds. Some is intentional and some simply natural; some is therapeutic and some tragic. Memory and forgetting perform an intricate, somewhat mystifying, dance through the course of the normal life experience, and sometimes even our memories can be a form of forgetting.

There is a short story from *The Book of Forgetting* by acclaimed Japanese writer Yasunari Kawabata, titled "Yumiura," which is well known to experts in memory due to the questions it poses about how fallible the normal human memory is. In the story, a middle-aged writer is visited by a woman who tells him in intimate detail that years ago they met in the town of Yumiura. She says that they became lovers and that Kozumi proposed to her during the Harvest Festival. Kozumi is distraught that he cannot recall her at all. How can she remember him so clearly? Is what she described true, or not? She is so certain of her memory that Kozumi begins to believe her—until he retraces his past and discovers he could not have been in Yumiura at that time. The story is fascinating to me because I could never convince myself of such a false recollection.

Kawabata's story is recounted in Dr. Daniel Schacter's important book *The Seven Sins of Memory,* in which he introduces seven primary mechanisms by which the normal human memory distorts reality. What was striking to me in reading about these seven mechanisms was that as far as I can tell, my mind doesn't seem to engage in any of them, though my recall hasn't been tested specifically by the scientists to evaluate that, so I can't be sure. These sorts of distortions and issues with memory seem alien to me. Scientists have also thrown up a thought-provoking and somewhat disconcerting mirror to the story of my life that has helped me to understand more deeply how the unusual workings of my memory have shaped my experience.

The first "sin" is what Dr. Schacter calls transience, which is the normal loss of memory over time. Apparently this normal memory loss begins within hours of the events forgotten. It's due to transience that most people remember many more things about what happened in the past few hours than about what happened the day before, and they remember even less about what happened on any given day of a week ago. An interesting question is whether this should be thought of as a weakness in normal human memory or in fact a strength, in that it clears the mind to focus on more important information. My mind just doesn't seem to work this way. As opposed to my memory growing weaker with age, it actually seems to keep growing sharper.

The second sin is absentmindedness. I've always marveled at the way people lose their ATM cards or can't find their keys or, when driving on the highway, suddenly come out of a fog and realize they've driven ten exit lengths without conscious thought or control. Some psychologists say that absentmindedness clears the way for our brains to be more creative, that the brain is working away on ideas while the mind seems to have checked out. I am never absentminded. I've never lost a single key. In fact I still have the house key my parents gave me when I was ten years old, which I used until I was thirty-seven, when we moved. I've never lost an ATM card or credit card, and I had the same driver's license until I was twenty-seven, when I had to renew it. I never find my mind wandering in this way; to the contrary, it's always crammed full of remembering. There are never times when the "film" isn't running and I can focus exclusively on the present moment.

One of the sins I find hardest to relate to is what Schacter calls blocking, which he describes as a tip-of-the-tongue feeling when you know you know something (like the name of an acquaintance or the answer to a trivia question) but you just can't get it out. For the period of my strong memory, from when I was fourteen on, I don't think I ever block the way he describes the sensation. Usually my memories come flying right out. For the earlier period when my memory was still developing, between about ages eight and fourteen, I sometimes have to think for a moment, but I don't have that tip-of-the-tongue sensation as I'm working on it.

Schacter calls these first three memory mechanisms "sins of omission." The four others he calls "sins of commission," which are a good deal trickier, even insidious. Misattribution is the sin when we remember doing things we didn't do, or jumble up our memories, like remembering that a friend was at a party when in fact you saw her for dinner the week before that, or thinking you've told one friend something when in fact it was a different friend you shared that story with. If you've ever watched an old movie that you absolutely clearly remember starred Gregory Peck only to discover when the opening credits roll that it stars Cary Grant, you were misattributing.

I found this a particularly intriguing distortion to read about, because I make note of the people in my life misattributing all the time and find it amazing, especially that they clearly really believe they're remembering correctly. I've learned that I have to stop myself from correcting people in most cases, which I used to do a fair amount of as a child. In fact, one of the facts about memory that Schacter reports is that people tend to privilege their own memories for events over the recollections of others. Most of the people close to me in my life pretty much gave up on doing that with me a long time ago.

It's hard to fathom how people's minds play this trick of misattributing, but an interesting theory about how autobiographical memories are recalled may go a long way toward explaining it. The theory is that our autobiographical memories are not stored all in one place in our brains; rather, we re-create them in an elaborate and delicate reconstruction process whereby different parts of an experience that have been filed away in different sections of our brains are pulled together again. This process is said to take up to 10 seconds, and it is vulnerable to errors. When we misattribute, we may be pulling together pieces of different experiences and fusing them into what seems to us to be a totally clear, accurate memory.

One of the sins that is most appalling to me is related but different; Schacter calls it suggestibility. This is the creation in our minds of outright false memories, such as through others' suggestions. The key is that the false recall comes from outside information, not from information stored away in our brains. Children are especially vulnerable to forming such false memories, as seen in a number of child abuse trials in which prosecutors unearth memories from children about sexual crimes that never happened. Not only is this false remembering damaging in such cases, it also raises serious issues in regard to eyewitness testimony in legal trials. Many studies have revealed that witness recall can be substantially flawed, in part due to the way in which the witnesses were questioned or shown information, such as in a lineup of suspects. As far as I know, my memory is not susceptible to suggestibility.

What seems to me one of the most problematic of the sins, because it is so subtle and so pervasive, is the one Schacter calls bias. This is the way that people's memory of the past can be significantly distorted by what they know or feel in the present. These distortions operate in many tricky ways, and Schacter identifies five key types. One, called consistency bias, causes us to make our thoughts and feelings more consistent over time, so that we remember feeling the same way about something in the past as we do now, even though we actually felt quite differently then. For example, someone who initially supported the Iraq War but now opposes it might misremember having ever supported the war. An example that Schacter describes is from one study that showed that if you asked a married couple how they had felt about each other five years earlier, they would tend to describe those feelings according to the way they were currently feeling, which, depending on the state of their marriage, might be a good thing or a bad thing.

Another category is change bias, which occurs when people think that they should have changed something in their lives or about themselves over time, and their minds exaggerate the actual amount of change that has happened. For example, if you attended an anger management class and think that you should have learned to become calmer, then you might exaggerate just how much improvement you've seen in your control over your temper due to the class. It's interesting that this bias can involve not only exaggerating how much better the situation is in the present, but also how bad the situation was in the past. To use the same example, a person might also exaggerate just how bad a temper she had before the class. The mind is endlessly creative!

One type of bias that is fairly easy to spot in friends and family is the distortion called hindsight bias, which is when people believe that they always knew something that they've in fact just found out about. With those who are close to us in life, this sort of rewriting of history is bound to come up fairly glaringly now and then. Say, for example, a friend who is a big fan of the Dallas Cowboys claims that he always knew they were going to lose a big game they'd been the strong favorite to win, even though you clearly remember him saying they were going to cream the other team. Schacter uses the case of the O. J. Simpson trial and how many people who had thought Simpson would be convicted said after the trial that they had known he'd be let off. Interestingly, this bias is much stronger when it seems to people, after the fact, that there was good reason for them to have had the correct view initially. If the difference in outcome seems due to a quirk of chance, then the distortion isn't nearly as strong. So if the quarterback for the Cowboys was injured, for example, then that friend who is a fan probably wouldn't be distorting about his prior expectation that the team would achieve a crushing victory, or at least not as much.

A type of distortion that has plagued human life in many ways that are all too obvious is that called stereotypical bias, which has been a contributing factor in racial and gender stereotyping. What happens in this process is that preordained, general views about a category of people are projected onto individuals. As Schacter writes, "Because it may require considerable cognitive effort to size up every new person we meet as an individual, we often find it easier to fall back on stereotypical generalizations that accumulate from various sources." Over time, this is one type of bias that I hope we can make serious headway in correcting.

The most personally damaging memory mechanism, in which people's memories turn against them, is known as persistence: people cannot forget disappointments or moments of shame in life, like failing a major test in school, or getting fired from a job, or being rejected by a lover. The rehearsal of these memories can cause great emotional harm, as when terrible memories like rape or abuse haunt people all their lives. The excessive replaying can even cause symptoms of post-traumatic stress disorder. Dr. Schacter refers to one case of persistence that led to shocking consequences—that of baseball player Donnie Moore, who was a relief pitcher for the California Angels. He was, as Schacter writes, "literally haunted to death by the persisting memory of a single disastrous pitch." Moore was brought in to finish off a game against the Boston Red Sox but ended up throwing a pitch that was hit out of the park for a game-winning home run. He ruminated about that pitch so persistently that he was driven into a terrible depression and ended up shooting his wife and then committing suicide by turning the gun on himself.

Research in the field of positive psychology, often called the science of happiness, has also produced powerful results about the negative psychological effects of ruminating, particularly in the onset of depression. Those who are depressive are more likely to ruminate, and those who ruminate are often dragged into depression. A horrible irony about this finding is that ruminators often think that their intense attention to whatever bad experience they're dwelling on will help them gain some valuable insights, when in fact, rumination tends to undermine critical thinking of that sort.

Although persistence would seem to be similar to my own memory, I don't think it is really the same as the kind of replaying that my mind does. My memory is not selective in that way, fixated on any particular event. For me, the least consequential moments persist alongside the most traumatic and influential. That's not to say, though, that my most upsetting memories haven't weighed especially heavily on me; they have, and they've thrown me into bouts of depression. It's just that the mechanism seems quite different to me, as I also have all kinds of inconsequential memories popping into my head in the same way all the time.

The ever-present nature of my memories about the slings and arrows of life makes me envy the way in which the last of the biases, which is called egocentric bias, distorts most people's memories in ways that are self-flattering. People tend to credit themselves more for successes than for failures, for example, and to privilege their successes in their memories of their lives. Psychologist Shelley Taylor, who has done important work on this subject, refers to this as creative self-deception. At the heart of egocentric bias is the tendency to put oneself at the center of the action in life, thinking that so many things have to do with us when they may not really be about us much at all. For example, we tend to interpret people's moods as having to do with our influence on them, when they may really be feeling that way because of something else entirely; or we tend to privilege our role in some joint task over the contribution of others. What is especially fascinating to me about the way that egocentric bias tends to distort our memories is that for most people, it ends up distorting things in their favor, so that they tend to "remember past experiences in a self-enhancing light," as Schacter writes.

Schacter argues that the "seven sins" have evolved over time because they are advantageous in many ways, or are the by-products of memory functions that have served us well. Through the long sweep of human history, they have been, in the words of evolutionary theory, adaptive. Egocentric bias, for example, can significantly improve well-being by making the past look a whole lot more successful or happy than it really was. I can't honestly say that I'd really want to have these "abilities," because I do like that my memory is so complete, though some egocentric bias would probably have done me a world of good. I also find myself wondering about the trade-offs in terms of knowing the truth about our lives. To me, accuracy about what has happened to me, about who said what when, and about the truth of a situation is vital. Interestingly, research in positive psychology shows that those who are natural optimists tend to remember their failures less accurately, seeing them in a relatively positive light. Research also shows, though, that their optimism, which has so many benefits, comes with a trade-off about realism, which in some circumstances, such as when it's important to be able to size up accurately a challenge being faced, can be problematic.

One of the most interesting questions about memory and forgetting is how much of each is optimal in our lives. The strength of the natural process of forgetting is remarkable to me. One study showed that over a period of 300 days, approximately 3 percent of life events were "highly memorable," which works out to about one event every three weeks. That sort of gap in the record of my life would truly disturb me. But then consider the case, fictional though it is, of the subject in Jorge Luis Borges's famous short story "Funes, the Memorious," which many people have said I would enjoy.

In the story, a teenage Argentinian boy named Ireneo Funes takes a bad fall while horseback riding and begins to have perfect memory. He remembers absolutely everything he sees and hears and reads in the finest detail. He remembers in such fine detail, in fact, that he has trouble sleeping at night, which has often been true for me, because he is rehearsing those limitless details in his mind. He can learn whole volumes of arcane information in mere days and develops an extraordinary facility for picking up foreign languages. He reads about historical cases of superior memory and marvels about what was so special in those cases because his memory is so much stronger than those people's were. So acute and complete did his memory become that, Borges writes, "he remembered the shapes of the clouds in the south at dawn on the 30th of April of 1882," and he "not only remembered every leaf on every tree of every wood, but even every one of the times he had perceived or imagined it." Tragically, Funes ultimately becomes lost in all of that detail, or, more accurately, imprisoned by it. He cannot free his mind from the minutiae he has become fixated by, and the narrator of the story conjectures that he has even lost the ability to truly think, because thinking requires being able to get perspective and to generalize, which Funes could no longer do. It is a strange and harrowing vision, and not insignificantly, Borges adds into the plot of the story that at the same time Funes was invested with his perfect memory in the fall from the horse, he became crippled.

I'm thankful that, complete as it is, my memory is not at all as fixated on details as was that of Funes, but the story is certainly thought provoking in terms of the ways in which my memory has ruled my life. In telling the story of my life in the rest of this book, it is in very large part the story of my memory that I will be relating, and I hope that in doing so, I shed some interesting light on that intricate, tricky dance of remembering and forgetting in all of our lives.

CHAPTER THREE

When I Was a Child

We could never have loved the earth so well if we had had no childhood in it.

—George Eliot, *The Mill on the Floss*

It is one of the great ironies of human experience that by the time we are old enough to reflect on what it is like to be a child, we are usually far removed from the experience.

—Stuart C. Aiken, *Playing with Children*

After the people are dead, after the things are broken and scattered . . . the smell and taste of things remain poised a long time, like souls . . . bearing resiliently, on tiny and almost impalpable drops of their essence, the immense edifice of memory.

—Marcel Proust, *Remembrance of Things Past*

One of the longest-standing notions in psychology is that even though we forget almost all of our earliest experiences, they shape us in profound ways, and one of the original goals of psychotherapy was to unearth those shaping experiences so that they could be intellectually and emotionally conquered. Although much of what Freud conjectured has been rejected by most psychologists, his central insight about early experiences playing a large role in personality development, and in continuing to influence us later in life, rings true to me, given my own life experience. Not only did the memories of my earliest years influence my life profoundly as I grew up, but they continue to do so. Given how vividly I recall a number of memories from between two and three years old, I certainly appreciate what the value of repressing might be.

I can still feel the irrational fears and unduly intense emotions about what—to adults—are in no way traumatic events, but kids are often horribly upset by. Remembering as many of my earliest memories as I do and as vividly as I do, I think that a great deal of the experience that becomes subconscious for most people has remained conscious for me. I've lived with a good deal of the roiling, irrational influence of what is normally driven into the subconscious right on the surface of my mind for my whole life.

What is your earliest memory? Perhaps you've known what that memory is for some time and can answer this question right away. It's true that at a certain point in our lives, our recall of our first memories becomes relatively fixed, though interesting research has shown that as late as in their twenties, most people's answers about what their first memories are still vary quite a bit from one time they're asked to the next. So, ask yourself again what that earliest memory is.

Stretch your mind back as far as you can go, and consider what your memory for the earliest years of your life is like. Maybe it's of a younger sibling showing up as a baby in the house or a bad fall. Those are common ones. Maybe it's something that scared you, like a dog barking at you, or something that confused you, like not being able to open a door in your house. Is it hazy? Is it a full event or just a fleeting moment? Maybe it's only a static vision of something, like a room in your home or a toy you loved. Can you hear anything that was being said to you or to someone else in the memory? Do you have any sense of smell associated with it? And do you feel any emotion when you recall it?

One of the most widely accepted findings in the science of memory is that about what's called childhood amnesia: the almost complete loss of autobiographical memory for the first two to three years of life. Yet scientists still don't know for sure why we forget these years.

Arguments about when the first long-term memories are formed in the brain differ. Some research has indicated that the brain may become capable of storing them as early as eighteen months. One study seemed to show that we may have some memory capacity even before we are born. In that study, mothers read aloud the same story passage repeatedly in the last months of their pregnancy, and when that passage was read to their babies in the first thirty-three hours after birth, they showed signs of recognizing it. But there doesn't seem to be any doubt that memories we may form from as early as that are ultimately lost. An interesting finding that seems to back up the assertion that it is at about eighteen months that infants begin to be able to remember is that this is also when they first demonstrate an awareness of a self. They recognize that they are looking at themselves in a mirror. But it doesn't seem to be until about twenty-two months that they develop a sense of self-consciousness, as we tend to think of our sense of self—to know that they are an individual in the world.

The range of age when the brain seems to develop in the ways that allow us to retain memories in the long term is generally between three and seven years, and a widely accepted argument is that long-term memory really begins at age four. Some people may have a few memories from before three years of age and some may not have any until even older than seven, but for many people, their first few memories are from between ages two and three.

The study of childhood amnesia is one of the truly fascinating areas of research in the science of memory, and I find the different theories about what causes it deeply thought provoking. Freud argued that it was due to the need to forget—or, to be more precise, to repress—traumatic early experiences. Some researchers have argued that it's due to the timing of the physical development of the brain, and that before certain structures are in place, memories can't be stored, at least not for the long term. But other work has suggested that the forgetting process is actually more significant—that it's not so much that we can't form memories at that age, but that our forgetting is in overdrive for this period. Still another theory is that we don't remember those years because we don't yet have language ability, and without language, autobiographical memories can't be encoded in our minds.

A theory that is especially intriguing to me, given the nature of my own earliest memories, argues that the reason we forget the first years is that the mind of an infant is different from that of an older child and an adult. An infant's understanding of the world is so undeveloped that the mind is not yet able to make sense of events in ways that allow episodic memories to be filed away. I can attest from my own recall that the infant mind is a wildly irrational one.

I do have childhood amnesia, but I also have a good number more memories from those earliest years than is normal. Some of them are intensely dear to me, and others can still send a shock of child fear and anger coursing through me.

My abiding overarching feeling for those early days is that I felt utterly loved in the warm cocoon of a close and caring family. There's no question that my memory of that time has played a powerful role in my life, both as a refuge that I retreat to and, I'm afraid, as an anchor that has in some ways weighed me down, keeping me tied firmly to a phase of life that most of us remember only quite vaguely and move on from without incessantly looking back.

I was born in 1965 at Mount Sinai Hospital in New York City to a close, loving, and protective Jewish family. Actually, "protective" doesn't even begin to describe it. When I was four years old, I had my tonsils out at Roosevelt Hospital, and my maternal grandmother insisted we take a taxi home, which seemed odd to me since we lived in the apartment building across the street. I remember wondering while I was being put into the cab why we weren't just walking. Family was a big part of my childhood in New York, and our apartment was always filled with relatives on both my mother's and father's side. For my first few years, I didn't actually realize they were from two different families.

We lived at the Coliseum Apartments—a complex of two apartment buildings on Fifty-eighth to Sixtieth Streets at Ninth Avenue, with a private garden in between the buildings. The garden was a magical place to me. It had thick green grass and was lined with walkways and benches and planted with rosebushes and big potted trees. All the preschool children played there during the day while the mothers talked and rocked their babies in their carriages. Our apartment had a wonderful view of St. Paul's Church across the street, and I loved the way its stone walls glistened in the sunshine. One of my favorite things to do was to climb up on the couch in our living room and look out the window at the view down Ninth Avenue to the Lincoln Tunnel; I was fascinated by how the roads and bridges crisscrossed. That view still means so much to me that eighteen years after we had moved away from New York, when I was in the city for Thanksgiving 1989, I took a friend to see our building and ended up standing in the middle of the street taking photo after photo down Ninth Avenue. To this day I still go to see the building we lived in every time I am in New York.

One reason that those earliest days have remained special to me is that they were also special to my parents. My mother says those days of the 1960s in the city were the best decade of her life because that's when she met my dad and had her family. They were deeply in love and were finding a new place for themselves in the world as my father's career as an entertainment agent started to take off. I loved hearing my dad talk about his work, and in the evenings, I couldn't wait for him to come home. Every night, I'd sit with him and my mother as he ate dinner and told her about his day.

Psychologists say that the stories our parents tell us about their own lives may have a significant shaping influence on us as we struggle to make sense of who we are, developing a concept of our own personalities. Our parents may also play an important role in what we end up remembering about our lives—what gets stored away in our long-term memories or what we tend to recall about our own lives. I know that for me, the stories that I heard about my parents' lives have meant a great deal to my sense of self, and I loved being taken into the story of their lives.

My father's family came from Newark, New Jersey, and he grew up there in the 1940s and 1950s, when lots of people who would go on to national acclaim, like author Philip Roth, were growing up close by, though he didn't know them. My grandfather owned a gas station in the Italian section of the city, which was strictly divided into enclaves by ethnic groups: Jews in one area, Italians in another, Poles in another. My father made quite a transformation in his life by getting into the entertainment business. He never made a conscious decision to go into the business; the notion was planted in his head by a friend one day, and my dad laughs when he remembers responding that maybe he could be an agent, because he didn't even know what an agent did. All he knew about agenting was what he had seen in the movies: the agent was the guy with the tattersall hat who went into a phone booth and made deals and got 10 percent.

At the time there were three big agencies—MCA, William Morris, and GAC. My dad managed to get interviews at all three and started off in the mailroom of William Morris, as all those aspiring to become agents for William Morris did. Within three months, he caught a lucky break that set his career into fast-forward. He was told to fill in for the sick secretary to one of the agents, Bernie Brillstein, who for decades was one of the biggest managers in the entire business and still commands a great deal of respect. Brillstein discovered Jim Henson and his Muppets, and later he handled Lorne Michaels and the *Saturday Night Live* comedians and writers. My dad had expected that he'd just be working for Bernie for a week or so until his secretary was better, but it turned out that the secretary didn't come back to work for four months, and those four months were an amazing time for my dad. Every Friday night, Bernie hosted a crap game at his apartment, around the corner from William Morris, and powerful people in the entertainment business would come by. My father started developing connections, and before long, Bernie had put him and two other agents in charge of a new commercials department at the agency. Though working with commercials wasn't as sexy as movies or TV, they managed a lot of young talent, like the Second City Players and actors like George Segal, who was just starting out.

I loved hearing about my father's clients as a young child, and spending time with him at work, and those early days with him are among my most cherished memories. At that age, when I was two through five, I didn't recognize any of the people he was talking about, including Ray Charles, one of my dad's clients who came to dinner once at our apartment. To me, Ray was just a very tall man with a wonderful smile standing in my living room, and—testimony to the fact that children's minds are not yet capable of making coherent sense of the world—I even suspected that he might possibly be my grandfather on my father's side. My grandfather had died before I was born, and all I really knew about him was that his name was Charles, so I asked Ray, "Are you my grandpa?"

The most fun for me about my dad's work was getting to go with him to the Ed Sullivan show. In those days, a younger agent was always assigned to escort the William Morris clients who were appearing on the show. This was a once-a-month duty, and the agent would stay with them while they rehearsed all day Saturday and Sunday until the show went live, at 8:00 P.M. on Sunday night. Often my dad would take me with him. First we would have breakfast at the Carnegie Delicatessen with a wonderful comedian known in the business as Fat Jack Leonard, who would always say to me, "Come here, little girl, you married? You're not married, little girl?" One of my favorite times watching the rehearsal at the Ed Sullivan show was when I was mesmerized by a magician practicing his magic act, but I was really more enamored by the assistant in her beautiful sequined dress than by his magic tricks. I thought the dress was so gorgeous that I told my dad, "Mommy should have a dress just like that." Every time Ed saw me sitting with my dad, he would come over and make a fuss over me. His son-in-law, the executive producer of the show, was really nice to me too, and he would bring a stool over to the side of the stage for me to sit on. Often I'd be sitting right next to Ed as the acts rehearsed.

My father's job as an agent not only made for an interesting childhood for me; it actually led to my birth. My mother and father met one day when my dad was working for an agent who represented the band leader Mitch Miller. He took some papers out to where Miller's show was shot in Brooklyn, at the Avenue M Studio, where silent movies had been made in the early days of film. *The Perry Como Show* was shot there too. The studio had two big stages, and Perry used one and Mitch the other. My dad went there to deliver some papers to a client, which he had volunteered to do because there were always pretty girls out there—all the shows' dancers.

My mother was working as a dancer on the Mitch Miller show at the time, and he met her there that day. She has her own interesting family story. Her mother, to whom she was extremely close, had come a long way from her roots in the little town of Waterloo, Iowa. From there, her family had moved to Baltimore, and the family story goes that they had picked up and moved at the suggestion of a Ouija board. They'd been thinking about going but couldn't decide, and when one day they took the board out and asked if they should go, the answer was yes, and that was it. When my grandmother was fifteen, she headed to New York, and somehow finagled her way into a Broadway show. She had taken two tap lessons in her entire life yet became a dancer in a show called *The Earl White Follies.*

My mom started taking tap lessons when she was nine, and later took classes at the school run by June Taylor, which is how she got the job dancing in Taylor's troupe. In the late 1940s and 1950s, the June Taylor Dancers appeared on lots of TV shows, such as the *Toast of the Town,* starring Ed Sullivan, and Jackie Gleason's *Cavalcade of Stars.* My mom started with Taylor when she was fifteen, and she was on the road all the time, doing shows at the Blue Room, the Shoreham Hotel in Washington, and in hotels in Lake Tahoe, as well as two of Guy Lombardo's Jones Beach shows, *Around the World in 80 Days* and *Paradise Island.* She also regularly did the Ed Sullivan show, the *Bell Telephone Hour*, and the Mitch Miller show, where she met my dad one afternoon.

My dad was so struck by her that when he got back to the William Morris office in Manhattan, he called and asked her to dinner. They both laugh when they remember that first date because he met her in Brooklyn, then went back to Manhattan to his office to call her, then picked her up back in Brooklyn, and they went back into Manhattan for dinner. And the back and forth still wasn't done. My dad had figured that she lived in Manhattan, but it turned out that she lived far out in Brooklyn, in Sheepshead Bay, with her mother. So after dinner, off they went back to Brooklyn, and he headed back to Manhattan one last time that night. They started dating steadily, and three weeks later he asked her to marry him.

My mom was, and is, beautiful, with dark hair and big hazel eyes and the slim figure and long legs of a professional dancer. But even from the time I was little, I always heard my dad say she was one of the most honest and strongest people he ever knew—very quiet but always with the strength inside her to do the right thing. This is one of the ways in which the stories my parents have told me from early on have influenced my life. Though both my parents worked with many celebrities, they always conveyed that it was most important to see the value inside people and not to be caught up in superficials or in the money culture.

I am extraordinarily grateful for the storehouse of warm memories that I have from our years in New York. Among my favorite family times are going out to dinner, almost every Sunday night, to Patrissy's, a restaurant in Little Italy. It had round tables and white tablecloths, and the waiters wore white jackets and black bow ties. In the front by the door was a huge lobster tank, and I watched the lobsters move around while we waited for our table. I always ordered the same thing: veal parmigiano. My parents let me bring my favorite doll with me, and I loved the place so much that I named her Patrissy. I dressed her in little infant one-piece yellow terry coveralls with a hood, and she always wore Pampers, which I insisted my mom buy for her when we went shopping. One of the things I like about my memory is that the pure happiness that I felt at those dinners is as alive and as gleeful in my mind today as it was then.

My early memories are apparently not only more numerous than most other people's childhood recollections, but are also clearer and fuller, and one of the pronounced features of my remembering, which seems to have developed by this early stage, is that I have heightened sensory perception in my memories. I hear the sounds, see the colors, and smell the smells of my memories much more vividly than most other people do when remembering, especially when they are remembering childhood. For some of those early memories, I love this quality of vividness, especially when I recall our summer vacations in Atlantic City.

From the time I was six months old until I was eleven, my family took a summer trip there and stayed at the Marlborough-Blenheim Hotel. Built in 1906, it was one of the grand old palatial hotels that lined the beaches in the decades before legalized gambling changed the whole complexion of the place. It was so big and opulent to my child's eyes that it remains my standard of wonder and luxury. The hotel had three buildings: a big white stucco section, a second of red and green wood, and a new section, built in the 1960s, that was very modern. The lobby was huge, and bridges connected the hotel buildings to the pool area, and tunnels led out to the beach. I loved the elegance of the beautiful carved mahogany bar in one room, and the library where musicians played violins at night, and how the bellhops wandered in and out announcing calls for guests. The place was a castle to me.

People dressed for dinner; my dad always wore a suit, and my mom and I wore dresses. There was something wonderful for me about being hot and sweaty all day and feeling the salt and sand on my skin, then bathing and putting on a clean white dress and my black patent leather Mary Janes and having my mom put my hair back. I had a little shoulder-length bob haircut and she would fix it with red barrettes and drape a sweater around my shoulders.

All the wonderful tastes, sounds, and smells of Atlantic City come to me when I travel back to those times, which I often do: the noise of people's shoes clunking on the boardwalk and the pinging of the games in the arcades; the pervasive smell of roasted peanuts, and that marvelous blend of the smells on the beach of suntan lotion and the ocean air. The Marlborough-Blenheim had its own distinctive smell; I smelled it in so many places in the hotel that the scent and the hotel became one and the same in my mind. Over the years, when I catch a whiff of that smell in other places, it sends me right back to the Marlborough-Blenheim. In 1992—Monday, November 30—when my mom and I were visiting our cousin Natalie in Florida, staying at her condominium, the three of us were coming up in her elevator, and I smelled that scent. I said, "Mom, doesn't it smell so good in here?

Doesn't it remind you of the Marlborough-Blenheim?" They looked at me a little strangely, and then my mother said to me, "Jill, that smell is mildew."

Though in many ways it's a great gift to be able to remember my childhood as vividly as I do, at the same time, many of the experiences of childhood—anyone's childhood—are emotionally distressing, and I remember those just as vividly. We don't often think of childhood as such, but it is a frightening time. My hunch is that our minds are built to forget so much of those years because we live them with intensity of emotion and a limited understanding of causality. We believe in monsters under the bed, see scary faces in the dark, and are never quite sure there isn't something hiding in the closet. I still feel the dark fear I had of the light switch in my parents' bedroom. At night if I sat up in my bed, I could see it, and it looked like a monster—no matter that during the day I would examine it and ask myself why I was so scared of it. I was three years old, and at night, it terrified me. I'm told most people look back on those irrational fears with none of that emotion left, and one of the crazy things about how my memory works is that I can't get that emotion, in all of its childlike intensity, out of my mind. I'm still the kid staring at that light switch in dread all over again. As much as I try to tell myself not to be silly, not to feel that fear, I cannot turn it off.

Another example of how my childhood emotions haunt me is one of my saddest memories, which I realize

I should not at all allow to still upset me. At one point, my dad took over as the agent for the amazing Muppet creator Jim Henson. Dad would tell stories about being at Henson's office when *Sesame Street* was just starting, and Henson would open up a drawer and there would be Kermit or Miss Piggy. My dad got such a kick out of Henson's studio that he arranged for my nursery school class to go visit, and I was thrilled. But I got very sick with tonsillitis a few days before we were to go. Of course, my parents still had to go because they were hosting the field trip, but being a kid I didn't understand and I felt cheated. I recall my mother standing in the dining room trying to explain to me why she had to go while I kept insisting that I had to go too. She says that despite my tonsillitis, she could hear me screaming at the top of my lungs all the way down in the elevator when she left.

It is a small thing in retrospect, and yet I recall it with an overwhelming sense of disappointment every time I see the Muppets, to this day. I think the reason we call experiences like being unable to visit the Muppets "small" is that for most people, they fade over time and are replaced by bigger problems or events certainly worth more attention than a missed school trip. It's not quite that way for me. I can still hear my mother's heels clicking down the hallway outside our apartment as she left, and to me, the feelings of that day are anything but small. Silly as it may sound, it is still not easy for me to see the Muppets today knowing that I missed meeting them many years ago. Of course, being unable to meet Big Bird and being frightened by a light are not high on the list of emotional traumas for most children—certainly not compared to a parent's death or divorce or any score of other tragedies. All of my life I have tried to use the perspective that time is supposed to give us to push the feelings of those memories away, but all this time they have persisted.

Probably my most traumatic childhood memories are ones of concern for my brother. Michael was born in November 1969, when I was three years and ten months old, and I adored him from the start. He has been a steadfast and deeply caring life companion for me—and my total opposite. Always independent, he struck out on his own early while I stayed at home, and he has gone on to a marvelous career as a TV producer. He has always been emotionally steady through all of our family turmoils, and from early on he has been a protector and a great comfort for me. One day when I told him I wished I had an older brother too, he told me, "That's okay, I'll be your big brother," and true to his word, he has always taken special care of me. When he was a baby, though, I was terrified that something would happen to him.

I found out a few months after I turned three years old that my mom was going to have another baby, and though I know some kids are wary about siblings joining the family, I was excited. I already knew that I wanted children of my own someday, and this would be almost like having my own baby. I took a lively interest in my parents' discussions about the baby, and when they told me they were considering naming him Mark, I told them that I wanted them to name him instead after my cousin Michael, whom I loved. To my delight, they agreed.

I remember the day well when my mom and dad left for the hospital. My grandmother stayed with me and brought me to the hospital later, after Michael was born. I was wearing red stockings with brown shoes and a little red skirt and sweater, and I was so excited to see my new brother. But the hospital staff made us sit in the lobby because little kids weren't allowed to visit the nursery. I still get mad when I remember that.

When we left, I stood on the street looking up at the hospital windows, and I was happy knowing that my baby brother was up there somewhere. When he came home, his day crib was in the living room, and I constantly checked on him. From the floor, I couldn't really see inside through the crib's bumpers, so I kept climbing up on one of the living room chairs to see in and check that he was still breathing. I could also crawl underneath, and I found a hole in the board under the mattress where I could stick my finger in and poke the mattress. If he moved around or made some noise, I was happy because that meant he was still alive.

The day of his bris, the Jewish ceremony of circumcision eight days after birth, was horrifying. The living room of our apartment was packed with people, and all I knew was that we were having a party for my brother. A strange-looking man with a beard came in carrying a Bible and what looked to me like a pouch of workman's tools. Everybody but me seemed to know why he was there. The mood was festive, but I could feel tension building, and I was suspicious about what was going on. Then all of a sudden I heard Michael scream, and the terror that I felt still rushes through me when I remember this. I tried to push my way through the forest of adult legs crowded around him, crawling in and out of the legs in a panic, looking for my mother. I vividly remember the smells of all the women's perfume, and I still feel my intense rage that no one would let me through. Finally I found my mother sitting in a chair looking shaken. I started patting her face and asking if she was okay, and even though she told me she was, I didn't believe her.

Later I was so worried about my brother that I kept asking to see him, but his baby nurse kept me away. Though I know it's irrational, I still feel resentment toward her when I go back to this memory. I was so annoyed about how she shooed me away. She had done the same thing when my mom and Michael had come home from the hospital. That day of the bris—the first time that I can recall she told me I couldn't see him—I consciously tried to force my memory back. I stretched to try and remember back to when I was born so I could recall my own baby nurse. My goal was to go back to when I was a week old so I could relive my own homecoming. I sat on the floor and kept concentrating, but I just couldn't go back that far.

Interestingly, one of the questions being studied about childhood memory concerns this issue of when children begin to forget the happenings of their lives. Does it start right away, or do children remember a good deal for several years and then later forget all of those memories? Research that would illuminate the answer to this question is difficult to devise, because until about age two, children can't speak, and for some time after that, they may not really understand the concept of a memory and what they are being asked to do when being asked to recall past events. But there is some evidence that young children's earliest memories are generally from earlier points in their lives than those of adolescents, and that adolescents, in turn, have earlier earliest memories than adults. So earliest memories are perhaps lost over time as opposed to not having been formulated at all. I think it would be fascinating for researchers to interview very young children in order to create a fuller understanding of how rich their memories are at that time. The idea that the memories might have been there for my mind to have captured more fully is intriguing.

My memories from years two to four are definitely spotty, more like how other people's memories are described to me than my memories for the later periods of my life. One distinct difference about my early memories, though, seems to be how vivid the emotion of them remains for me. Although some research has shown that the specific emotion felt at the time a long-term memory was encoded is not stored along with that memory, it seems that in my brain, the emotion does get stored.

Another early memory of mine regarding Michael is particularly intense this way. When I was four years old, my mom took me down to the garden between the two buildings of our apartment complex and said I could play there alone because she had to be upstairs with Michael. She was firm that as soon as she came back down to the lobby door and put her hand up, I had to come running. That was the first time I was given so much freedom, and I played happily in the dirt beside the privet hedges, with a blue pail and yellow shovel that I loved. The trouble came after she came and got me. The key jammed in our front door lock, and as my mother fiddled with it, I panicked, running up and down the hallway yelling, "We have to get to Michael!" My mother finally got the door open, and I ran straight to Michael's bedroom, terrified that he might be hurt, but of course, he was perfectly fine, holding on to the side of his crib and jumping up and down smiling.

When I remember this incident, I am jolted by that utterly irrational fear that I felt about Michael, and the clarity with which I still feel my earliest memories has given me great sympathy for what children that age go through. When I see a small child crying uncontrollably or having a temper tantrum, I am sent right back to those intense days myself.

The scientists who studied me do not know exactly how the nature of my memory has affected my emotional makeup. Because my memory syndrome is so little understood and because the science of the ways in which our earliest memories influence our lives is still developing, it's impossible to know in a truly scientific way how the lingering emotions of those earliest childhood experiences have changed my psychological development. I have no doubt, though, that the way that I've retained so many of these intense childhood fears has had a profound effect on my life. In particular, I cannot remember a time when I haven't had a terrible dread of death, and I've also had a compulsion about order. I believe both stem from a particular memory, from when I was two, when I overheard a conversation between my mother and her friend Diana.

My mom recently mentioned Diana, and how her father had died a long time ago and I said, "Oh, I remember that." She balked, saying I couldn't possibly remember that, and so I told her the story of my memory. "It happened when I was two years old. You and Diana were talking in the living room . . ." My mom and Diana and a third friend of theirs, Patty, were talking about Diana's father having gone into the hospital for surgery and died. What stuck most in my mind was that they kept saying he had "wrapped things up" and "got things in order," which evoked an image in my mind of him sitting at some old desk and locking things up as he put them away. I wasn't sure why he would do that, but it seemed the only thing alleviating how upset they were that Diana's father was never coming back: he got his things in order. As I try to trace the arc of my life, it seems to me that along with that image of Diana's father putting his affairs in order, I developed an enduring fear of death and also of disorder. To my child's mind, the associations were simple: someone is dying—bad. Putting things in order—good. That simple child logic still holds sway over me.

Though I would never want to lose my wonderful memories of my earliest years in New York, I wish the intense feelings of fear and confusion, anger and dread, that my mind still conjures up so vividly from those days had dissipated as they normally do. I'd absolutely love to be able to remember the good and forget the bad.

As I've reflected on how the fact that my mind has stored so many memories starting so early has affected my life, I've come to realize that one of the most profound ways is that I have not really wanted to leave the past. For whatever reason, and somewhat ironically, from early on, I came to hate the idea of change. I never really felt excitement about new stages of my life as I know so many people do at junctures in their lives, such as when graduating from college. I never wanted to move on to new things, at least not until I met my husband.

I think I would have liked to stay in our apartment in

New York with my mom and dad and brother and all our relatives and my dad's clients coming over all the time for the rest of my life, and I intensely envy people who have lived in the same home their whole lives. Before long, I was to move away from New York to the suburb of South Orange, New Jersey, and though that first move was not unduly upsetting, at some point in my years in South Orange, I developed a profound attachment to my home there. When my family later moved from there to Los Angeles, the trauma of that move may well have played a role in the way my memory began to intensify not long after.

CHAPTER FOUR

The Remains of the Days

Home is the place where, when you have to go
    there, they have to take you in.
I should have called it
Something you somehow haven't to deserve.
    —Robert Frost, "The Death of the Hired Man"

The old saying "home is where the heart is" does not even begin to express the degree of attachment I have felt to my homes. In fact, I have never left home. I was in the process some years ago of moving out on my own, to live with the man I'd fallen in love with and married, but that's a story I'll save to tell later.

Early on, I became so deeply rooted to home that the thought of moving from my house absolutely terrified me. I also early on became intensely attached to what I call the artifacts of my life, from toys to records to notes from friends, and what was to become a vast storehouse of mementos. It seems that these two phenomena are interrelated: the need to keep things and the need to stay in the same place have been, I think, different facets of the intense dread I've had about change.

There is an odd irony about this. Although I remember the days and places and conversations and events of so much of my life so well, from early on I have felt an urgent desire to hold on to those days and places and events—and also to the things of my life. I can't say exactly why this is true, but I have found that holding on to the artifacts of my life gives me great comfort. Having actual things that are attached to the memories swirling in my head seems to make the strangeness of living in the past at the same time as the present less surreal.

The irony of wanting to keep a hold on the places and the artifacts of my life makes me think about the great *Twilight Zone* episode about a man who loves to read so much that he just wants to escape from life so that he can read all day. One day he goes down into a bank vault to hide away and read while he should be working, and he is the only survivor of a nuclear Armageddon. When he comes out of the vault, the landscape around him is a wasteland, and he's alone. At first he's delighted, because he'll get to read as much as he wants, but then he trips and his glasses fall off, and while he's looking for them, he steps on them and crushes the lenses. There he is, with all the time he ever wanted for reading, and now he can't see.

My memory means I don't need photographs to remind me of how my family and friends and my houses and home towns looked when I was growing up or to call to mind my favorite vacations and holidays. I can travel back to any home I've lived in and remember it vividly— taking it with me, in effect, when moving to a new one. Though one would think that would give me all the freedom in the world from any need to keep mementos or to keep a diary of key life events, it's just the opposite.

When I was three, I began to collect all the important items of my life, almost all of which I've kept. These included a small army of dolls, from a beloved collection of Madame Alexander dolls and Barbies, to the Sunshine Family and Dawn dolls, as well as the beloved doll carriage I received as a gift when I was seven. Then there is my host of stuffed animals, including 150 Beanie Babies. I amassed a treasure trove of Cinderella records and books, as well as a horde of Flintstones memorabilia— anything Flintstones that I could get my hands on back in the 1970s. I've kept every record I was ever given or bought—my first 45 was Jim Croce's "Bad, Bad Leroy Brown." I have all the Golden Books my parents gave me, as well as the little white rocking chair that the William Morris Agency gave to my parents the day I was born. Though it may seem an odd memento, I've also kept one of my dresser drawers from when I was five; I loved that dresser.

In 1982 I started to make tapes of songs off the radio that I labeled meticulously by season and year, and I kept that up until 2003. I still have all of those tapes. In late 1988, I started making videos of TV shows, and I have a collection of close to a thousand of them. I also started an entertainment log in August 1989 in which I wrote down the name of every record, tape, CD, video, DVD, and 45 that I own.

My obsession about keeping things even extended for a while to making some record of everyone who had visited our house. In sixth grade, I decided that I wanted anyone who came over to our house to sign an autograph book I'd been given. For the next couple of years, all those who walked into my house would be asked to sign it.

My parents have always been understanding about my need to keep things, allowing me to fill my bedroom full of my "collection." In October 1991 I took over my brother Michael's room when he moved out, and filled it full too. To anyone but me, my room probably looked like an attic, though it was important to me that everything was kept in a strict order, and my room was never a mess. I arranged my dolls in a specific way on my bed and my bookshelves; even when I put them in the stroller and walked them around the streets of New York, I had to make sure they were in the same order every time.

Five years ago my parents finally convinced me to move most of my collection into a storage unit when they were moving out of the house I lived in for twenty-seven years in LA. We rented a large storage container, and I was packing all of my things up for weeks, which was horribly stressful and upsetting, though ultimately I think it has been good for me, and I still know exactly where everything is. As I reflect on what my parents have put up with, I am grateful that they were so accommodating of this obsession of mine.

When it came to moving, my need for rootedness and for holding on to the physical situation of my life was harder for them to accommodate. It didn't start out that way. When I was five years and three months old, in early 1971, my family moved from Manhattan to South Orange, New Jersey, and reflecting on that move now, considering how traumatic moving became for me later, it's almost miraculous to me how readily I adjusted.

My brother was sixteen months old and growing fast, and the New York apartment was getting a bit tight for all four of us. The idea of moving out of the city wasn't particularly upsetting to me, and I was excited to go with my parents when they took me and my grandmother with them to see a house in South Orange. That house was a beautiful three-story red brick colonial with big windows framed by black shutters, and several large trees in the front yard, with a flagstone walkway leading from the sidewalk to the front door. We had a big entry area and foyer, with a spiral staircase, and a lovely dining room, with a swinging door into the kitchen that was painted an incredibly bright and cheery yellow. We also had a great den, with brown shag carpeting (so '70s) and a guest room on the first floor where Michael and I watched endless hours of TV.

I fell in love with the house immediately, especially my bedroom. It was a good-sized square room, with pale yellow walls and plenty of space for all of my furniture and toys. I was especially delighted by a set of built-in shelves where I could arrange my dolls, pictures, and books in just the order I liked to keep them. The basement had a huge playroom and a bar room with a restaurant-style bar and a table and booth with red cushions on the seats. The attic, magical to me, had pull-down steps in the upstairs hallway, and I'd go up there and hang out amid the boxes of our things packed away. The smell of that attic is dear to me.

The day we went to see the house, it was snowing, and my grandmother had me so bundled up that I could hardly see through the red wool scarf she had tied around my neck and most of my face. I had another of those little childhood traumas that day. As the adults walked through the rooms, I decided to take a look around for myself, and when I walked out a back door, it locked behind me.

When I tried to get back in, I thought I must have tried the wrong door, and I panicked and ran around the house twice before my dad found me.

The small school I attended was behind our house, and our backyard was enclosed by a fence with a gate that led right to the yard of the school. One of the best things about the house was that backyard. I had loved the garden at our apartment building, but this was going to be ours alone. It was rimmed with trees, and we had a swing set and lots of room to play. Moving into that house was the only time in my life that I have felt excited about a new place to live.

I did go through a bit of sadness as we were packing the New York apartment. I remember sitting with my dad on the rolled-up carpet in the New York living room watching the movers and saying to him, "Well, I guess we're really doing it." My dad was completely happy about the move, but my mom and I both had a combination of excitement and sadness, and the first night in the new house my mom cried, which started Michael and me crying too. But we all adjusted quickly.

Our neighborhood was full of kids, and a group of seven of us played all the time: three Roberts, Judy, Jeffrey, Michael, and me. We played Running Bases, Red Rover, and games we just made up at the moment. Backyards are like individual magic kingdoms to children, and we had our own mythical Middle Earth to play in.

One of the things I remember most vividly about

South Orange is the distinctive musty smell, which was particularly strong during the hot summer months. I love it when those summer days pop into my head. When I returned to New Jersey in August 1986 and again in August 1996, there was that familiar musty smell, and it brought me right back to those days playing in my driveway and running wildly around my backyard.

I had a harder time adjusting to school than I did about moving to the house. When I started at Newstead School in April 1971, I was at the end of kindergarten. I was the "new girl," and even though my class had only eight kids in it, I was desperately shy and spent the first three weeks hiding in my cubby. My teacher, Mrs. Mc-Griff, was a wonderful educator who understood about children's lives. She recommended to my mom that she invite my class to my house to have cookies and get to know me, and I remember vividly how proud I was to show everyone where I lived. Then, to celebrate Flag Day, my class put on a play, *The Big Birthday,* and Mrs. McGriff made me the star of the play. From then on, I loved that school.

Because I was blissfully happy in those years in South Orange, I was distraught when I learned at eight that we were going to be moving to Los Angeles. Any child feels dread about moving, of course, even if it's just to a new school, not a new town or state. We tend to think that children readily get over that sort of trauma. Some people may even think that moving during childhood is good for kids, helping them to develop social skills and learn to accept change and adapt. That may well be true for most children. For me, the experience was wrenching, and I think it had long-term impact. A fascinating question about why that has been true is whether it was due to the way my memory was already developed by that time, causing me to be so rooted to place and to hate change so much, or whether the trauma I experienced from the move perhaps exacerbated in some way the workings of my memory.

Scientists don't know why my memory changed at this time—whether it was due to some sort of physical development that was programmed into my brain's growth genetically or was perhaps caused by the emotional trauma of the move. Given that my brain scans show that my brain has some structural features that are a great deal different from the norm, perhaps my memory functioning was developing in certain ways by that time. At this point in the study of my memory, it's impossible to know. All I know for sure is that it was after our move from South Orange that the first big change in my memory happened, and my mind started to fill up more and more with memories.

When I think about our move to California, it's clear enough to me intellectually that I should have been thrilled to go, especially since I had enjoyed visits out to LA so much for the year before we actually moved. My father was offered a job at Columbia Pictures Television, at the Burbank Studios, as an executive in charge of television production, a dream opportunity for him. For a year, he lived in LA on his own, staying at the Beverly Hills Hotel, and my mother, Michael, and I visited him regularly.

I loved those trips, and I had no idea that after that first year, we were going to move to LA too. Dad usually stayed in a regular room at the hotel, but when we came to visit, he would get a bungalow for us. We would hang out at the pool and see lots of celebrities, and though I'd grown up meeting celebrities, this was more exciting because it was Hollywood and so glamorous. I also got to know lots of the children of celebrities. During one stay I hung out a lot with Neil Sedaka's daughter, and on another I chummed around in particular with Red Buttons's daughter. A man named Sven ran the pool. He was a beautiful blond guy who wore white shorts and a white shirt and made sure that we always had the same chairs around the pool.

The hotel and grounds were so safe that Michael and I were allowed to roam freely during the day. I felt like the character Eloise, the star of a series of children's books about a little girl who lived at the Plaza Hotel and got into all sorts of mischief. The hotel felt like my second home. I loved getting into bed and always having clean, cold, new sheets, and the smell and the feeling of them. I also especially loved going to breakfast downstairs and then heading to the gift shop to buy Reeds, candies like Lifesavers. The first time I was in that shop, I bought a map to the movie stars' houses, which I still have. I also loved just sitting in the lobby and watching the uniformed man who was always there. He would call out to people who had a phone call or a message, walking around with a sign and saying, "Calling Mr. Smith, calling Mr. Smith . . ."

My mom would take us shopping sometimes too, and I was in awe of the boutiques on Rodeo Drive. One time we had finished shopping in Beverly Hills and were eating at the restaurant Nate 'n Al's, and Milton Berle just walked right over to the table and grabbed my cheeks and squeezed them and told me how cute I was. My grandmother, who came out to LA with us often, was such a fan of his that she told me I couldn't wash my face for a week because Milton Berle had pinched my cheeks.

Among my favorite things to do when we visited LA was to go to Burbank Studios with my dad. The walls in the hallway were lined with pictures of all the Screen Gems shows like *I Dream of Jeannie* and *Bewitched,* and I spent hours walking up and down those halls looking at them. The most special day there was when I saw David Cassidy. For two years, I had had a huge crush on him, and I had made my dad take me to see him in concert at Madison Square Garden. There I was at the Burbank Studios one day, wandering around the Columbia offices by myself, and I heard someone behind me. Instead of turning around to look, I bent down and looked backward between my legs, and who was it? David Cassidy. I let out a shriek and took off running.

I also loved playing on the lot of Burbank Studios, especially on the set of *The Waltons,* a show I watched religiously. I would swing on the swings and feed the chickens, and run gleefully around the house, which was just a facade and floor. I was a wonderfully fortunate child, and I so wish that I had been happy about actually moving out to California. But when the time came, I was devastated.

In the spring of 1974, my parents decided that all of the travel back and forth was too difficult, and we moved into a rented house in LA, but even then I thought the move was only going to be temporary. I was still terribly upset that I had to move most of my collection into our attic in South Orange because my parents had rented our house out to another family. I could live with this situation because I knew all of my things were protected, and it was only going to be for a year. Then we were going to be moving back to New Jersey and I could put everything back in place.

The moment that I was told that we were going to be staying in LA is one of my most emotionally upsetting early memories. I was in the bathtub in my parents' bathroom of our rented house in LA in April 1975 when I got the news. I was washing with a bar of Irish Spring, which may be the reason I hate the smell of that soap. My mom came in and told me we were not going back to New Jersey and were going to be buying a house in LA. I was distraught. That was the most traumatic moment of my young life, and it was at this time that I started to truly obsess about how happy I'd been in New Jersey and New York. I started making lists of my friends from back east, constantly looking at pictures of our New Jersey house and thinking about the past all the time.

For whatever reason, right after I got to LA, I began to develop much more complete and vivid memories. From July 1, 1974, on, I remember in much more detail. I was eight, and I know—and have always felt, even then—that my memory underwent a deep and basic change of some kind.

The move was grueling. I was upset all the time in those last days in New Jersey and my friends were upset too. The night before we left the house, my mom, Michael, and I sat in my mom's room crying because we didn't want to leave. I felt my world was shattering. My friends gave me a going-away party, and my present was a little phone book, with a cover that looked like blue jeans, with my name on it. They had put all their addresses and phone numbers in it, which made it the perfect gift for me. I crammed that and all sorts of mementos from New Jersey into a camel-colored corduroy pocketbook and took to thinking of the contents of that pocketbook as all my worldly possessions from New Jersey. I put notes from friends that I'd saved in it, lists of names of my friends, pictures that I'd drawn of my house, a set of photos of all the rooms in the house that my mom took for me, and photos from my going-away party. I felt that I had captured my life in New Jersey in that little purse, and I still have it, still crammed full of all of those artifacts of a time I still find special. To have those lists of names and pictures and notes made me feel that I had the people still with me, and from then on, it has been important to me to keep all sorts of mementos of that kind.

In 1996, twenty-two years after we had moved from South Orange, I went back to see my old neighborhood and took twenty-eight rolls of film of the house and the streets and even the road signs so I could have a physical record of all of that. I often say that my ideal life would have been to have lived in the same house for all of my years, and I envy the people who have done so. Although we moved into a wonderful house in LA and I had enjoyed my visits there so much, I knew that my life would never be the same. In part because I had come to abhor change so much, adjusting to my new life in LA was a real struggle.

I've always felt that the trauma of moving to California was related in some way to the way my memory began to strengthen so much not long after, so I was fascinated to learn about a phenomenon known as the memory bump. Though the general rule about forgetting is that we do so more and more as time goes on, one of the big surprises in memory research is that there is in fact a spike in autobiographical memories for the years between ages ten and thirty. The memories during this bump also tend to be more vivid.

What especially fascinated me about this finding is that it was at about this age when my memory started to shift gears. But my memory didn't just bump, it went into overdrive and has never slowed down. Not long after we moved to California, my memory started to swirl out of control in my head. That happened in two stages—one when I was eleven and then again when I was fourteen.

As with so much of memory science, there are varying theories about what causes the bump. One is that we have many more emotional and novel experiences in our lives during these years, and in middle age to later years, we are more accustomed to so many experiences. Many people remember the first time they had sex, for example, but as they get older, they don't remember particular instances of having sex nearly so well. Another idea is that our brains simply have more memory power during these years, consolidating long-term memories better. The most interesting explanation to me is that most people have more memories from this time period because it is in these years that we are generally formulating and fixing in our minds our sense of self, and memory and self are closely intertwined.

An intriguing question about this relationship is which way it goes: Do we develop a sense of self because we begin to store more long-term autobiographical memories, or do we develop more memories from this time because our minds have evolved a firmer sense of self, which selects for the experiences we remember?

Adults past this age may have new bumps later in life if their lives are powerfully disrupted in some way, such as by divorce. They may at that time go through a process of, in some ways, creating a new life for themselves, and to an extent craft a revised sense of identity, and this may cause them to encode into long-term memory a higher quotient of memories once again.

Though it has always seemed to me that the reason my memories began to swirl so wildly through my mind stemmed from the trauma I felt about the move to California, perhaps it has more to do with my brain having developed in certain ways at this time, along the lines of growth that might explain the memory bump. The most thought-provoking insight to me about the memory bump is this notion that more memories get firmly stored away at this time because we are launching into the major enterprise of working out our sense of self—of who we are as an individual person, apart from our families and friends.

I think the fact that I have such especially strong recall from these first years of the process of self-building backs this theory up powerfully, because the memories I've retained from those years have been intensely self-defining. They were difficult years, and because I remember them so well, I can say perhaps with more certainty how they've shaped my psyche. I've often wondered whether my sense of self would have developed entirely differently if we had never moved to California. I can never really know for sure. The question is one that would haunt me through the next phase of my life, which I call my "roller-coaster years."

CHAPTER FIVE

The Stuff Our Selves Are Made Of

One of the striking facts of most lives is the recurrence of threads of continuity, the re-echoing of earlier themes, even across deep rifts of change.

—Mary Catherine Bateson, *Composing a Life*

It is only starting with adolescence that Mnemosyne begins to get choosy and crabbed.

—Vladimir Nabokov, *Speak, Memory*

I read an article in *The New York Times* a while back by psychology reporter Benedict Carey in which he wrote, "Every American may be working on a screenplay, but we are also continually updating a treatment of our own life." Constructing a life story, and continually re-crafting that story, the article went on to explain, helps a person to define herself, work out what sort of person she thinks she is, make choices about important life decisions such as what career to pursue, and discover a sense of the purpose or meaning in her life. As Carey also wrote, these life stories, when people are asked to write them down, tend to break down into episodes, along the lines of chapters, written in outline form, and they emphasize a key set of pivotal or defining experiences centering around what are called self-defining memories.

An explosion of work has been done in recent years in the study of how autobiographical memory is crucial in the shaping of people's life stories, particularly during the school years and into what is called emerging adulthood, in the twenties. As one of the leading researchers in this area writes, "Because the life story is constructed from significant memories that are connected into a coherent, ongoing narrative, autobiographical memory is the raw material from which identity is constructed as a life story."

The argument is that one's sense of self depends in large part on autobiographical memories—not only on the actual memories but also on the meaning attached to those memories and the lessons a person thinks she has learned from them. As the authors of one thought-provoking paper on the subject write, "Our knowledge of self is very much tied up with the 'story' of how what we have experienced has made us who we are, and how who we are has led us to do what we have done."

Interestingly, it's just about the same time that the memory bump begins, around ten years of age, that we seem to start to learn how to tell good stories about our lives, to recount events that have happened to us in coherent ways. As anyone who has been told a story by a young child can attest, kids younger than age ten generally don't know how to weave a good tale; they often ramble on without any real point or punch line. The development of the storytelling ability seems to go along with the process of constructing the very story of who we are.

But it's not during the elementary and middle school years, research suggests, that we begin to truly craft this story; it's only as we head into later adolescence and early adulthood that we begin to derive what will become guiding lessons about life and about ourselves from the memories we've stored, privileging a certain set for special emphasis—those called self-defining memories— while culling out a huge number of others. This offers a persuasive explanation about why adolescence is such a roiling, tempestuous time; young people at that age haven't quite fully constructed their sense of self, and their identities feel vulnerable, even under siege at times, and the process of beginning to determine who you think you really, *truly* are can be excruciating. It certainly was for me, and remembering those days vividly, I have enormous sympathy about the process.

This shaping of a life story is not a conscious process, like writing a story, though a good deal of conscious reflection may be involved. For some people, that reflection unfortunately intensifies into rumination, which can lead to deep depression and even suicidal thoughts. Far too many adolescents commit suicide, and this struggle with the crafting of a firm and empowering sense of self may well be an important contributing factor.

Though we don't simply choose what our life story will be, it is tailored in ways that give our memories of our lives a sense of meaning, and the memories that are recalled in support of our life story also vary over time. As one article about this research explains, "If you ask college students to tell you their most important memories, and then surprise them six months later by asking again, they will repeat stories at a rate of just 12 percent."

This new emphasis on memory itself as a shaper, not just a record, of our identities is a fascinating complement to other theories of the forces that make us who we are, such as about genetics and the effects of parenting styles. One of the most interesting aspects of my memory is the way in which it throws light on these new ideas about memory and the life story versus those other theories.

Those elementary and middle school years, and all the way through adolescence, are a crucible. We often feel that the smallest slight from a friend, or the taunts that kids have such unlimited creativity about hurling, are devastating wounds. Our emotions are raging at this age, and we fly off the handle and sulk and become irrationally upset regularly. Anyone with children this age knows this well. I remember it well from my own life.

I know from talking with my friends through the years that plenty of people do retain some memory of the pains from those middle childhood days. But most people's minds clear themselves of the vast majority of them. Even while we are young, normally our minds are constantly clearing themselves of the traumas of these experiences. If you ask a child about a temper tantrum she had a few years before, or remind him about how he was frightened of swimming in the deep end of the pool, she or he may well not remember those things at all, and almost certainly won't have the same view of them as they did at the time.

Most people put these times into perspective as they mature. Some good research has shown that the way people most often process these negative childhood experiences into memory is to derive positive lessons out of them, crafting them into nuggets of life wisdom. There is also a good deal of selective forgetting about them. Of course, some people focus more on negative memories in crafting their life stories, and derive self-undermining rather than empowering lessons from them, and that leads to a great deal of trouble in life.

That's a powerful testament to what a wonder it is that the human brain seems to have such a natural procliv-

ity for privileging the positive in building memory. A remarkable finding about the memory bump that begins at
age ten and backs this up is that the spike in memories
seems to be much more for positive times than for negative ones, confirming that usually, many more of the positive experiences during this phase of life make their way
into long-term memory than negative ones. Exactly why
this is the case hasn't yet been established and may never
be agreed on. Do we actually lay down fewer negative
memories than positive ones, or does our memory privilege the positive ones in the process of recall? Scientists
don't know.

I can say unequivocally, given the richness of my own
recall for this period, that it surely is one of the greatest
gifts of forgetting that most of that emotional turmoil becomes hazy over time in most people's minds, if not completely forgotten. In this regard, my memory is entirely
different. It did not seem to select for the positive in this
way as I began the process of constructing my life story,
which I think has contributed greatly to the negative self-
image I began to develop during these years. My sense is
that this is one of the most profound ways in which my
memory has shaped me: those roiling middle childhood
days continue to haunt me on a daily basis. I believe that
had my memory been normal, I would have had a wonderfully happy life.

After all, we had a great life in LA in so many ways,
and my brother, Michael, fell in love with the place right

away. My parents bought a lovely French country–style ranch house in the Encino section of Los Angeles with a large backyard planted with flower gardens and a pool, which I hung out at for untold hours with my friends. The house and yard were so striking that people regularly rang our doorbell asking if we would consider selling the house. My favorite thing about our house was my bedroom, which looked like a room in a doll's house. It had a peaked ceiling with exposed beams and a window seat with cushions and pillows, and the windows were framed by white shutters. It even had a matching bedspread and drapes and wallpaper that I loved, with a floral print in pink and blue and green and yellow—a perfect girly hideaway.

I did come to enjoy a good deal about the LA lifestyle. For one thing, my parents loved to give parties, and for the first couple of years, we had one at the house almost every weekend. My parents had already developed a large circle of friends during the time we'd spent in LA, and they were like a big extended family for us. We also went to the beach all the time, often with the family next door. Their son, Gregg, was just four months younger than me, and their daughter, Stephanie, was just five months older than Michael. The four of us became inseparable. I can see how my life might have evolved at this point; it should have been absolutely fantastic.

I ought to have gotten over the pain of the move from Jersey fairly quickly, had a great life as a teenager—

though with the normal ups and downs of those years—headed off to college looking forward to a new adventure, and then fallen in love and started a family, as I'd been intent on doing even as a young child. I might well also have pursued a great career as an entertainment producer, which I thought at times I might like to do. That's much too simple for a life story, of course, but as an abstract outline, it's a life I might well have had. When I got to adolescence, though, and the process of shaping an empowering, fundamentally positive sense of self should have kicked in, it seems that in large part because of the way my memory works, things didn't happen that way for me. I was not able to privilege positive memories, and those elementary and middle school days haunted me at the time I should have been stepping back from them and crafting a forward-looking and esteem-building life story. They haunt me still.

When I started school in California, I went through culture shock. I was in the fourth grade when we moved, and the school my parents enrolled me in was much bigger than any other school I'd gone to. In both New York and New Jersey, I had attended small schools. At my school in South Orange, there were only seven others in my class. Now I was thrown into a class of 134, and I had my first encounter with the childhood scourge of cliques. Getting a read on who was popular and who was not, and the whole notion of popularity, and then figuring out the rules of the game was a nightmare. I felt utterly lost, and I found myself thinking about New Jersey almost constantly.

Often after school I'd sit in our backyard looking out over the valley and think about those days. I was never able to put them behind me and make the kind of break that most other children do fairly readily, maybe after a first few really tough months, when they move.

On top of feeling rooted to New Jersey, I began to find my classes a struggle, I think in large part because, as the scientists were to confirm later, my mind was bad at the kind of memorization that becomes so important in school at this time. My mind doesn't memorize well, especially not the kinds of facts that make up so much of what kids learn at that age, and I find it hard to focus on things that don't genuinely interest me.

One of my most painful memories from this time is of my parents telling me that one of my teachers had said to them that I needed to "have a fire lit under me," because I was lazy about my schoolwork. I think I appeared lazy because I was frustrated by the assignments, and I probably seemed not to be applying myself. The worse I felt about leaving New Jersey, the more I withdrew into myself, and into my memories, during those first two years.

I did have one almost magically good year of school, in sixth grade. My parents sent me to a new school that year, St. Michael's and All Angels Parish Day School, much more the kind of school I'd been used to. My class had only eighteen children, and I was well prepared for the switch because the summer before, my parents had enrolled me in St. Michael's summer school. I thrived at St. Michael's, and to this day I carry that year very close in my heart.

My teacher, Miss Drew, had just graduated from Smith College, and this was her first class. She had lots of energy and was full of fun ideas about how to teach. When we studied colonial history, for example, she brought in a big antique sewing machine and showed us how to make clothes with it. She even took us on an overnight camping trip out to the Angeles National Forest. The only thing I was a little worried about at St. Michael's was that I had to go to chapel every day. Being Jewish, that was totally alien to me, and my ten-year-old mind was a little nervous that God might be angry at me. What was a Jew doing in church? But I grew to love going. The chapel was so quiet and serene that it relaxed me. In all ways, St. Michael's was a sweet school, and to this day I often travel to it in my memory for comfort.

The next school I went to was its opposite. Because St. Michael's went only through sixth grade, my parents had to find a new school for me. I took the entrance exams for several of them, and because of its reputation, my parents chose the Westlake School for Girls in Holmby Hills, California, the sister school to Harvard Boys School. Westlake had been around since the turn of the century, and it was a close community where the headmaster regularly reminded us that we were one and united together. Lots of children of celebrities went there when I did, such as Neil Simon's daughter Nancy; Charlton Heston's daughter Holly; Michael Landon's daughter Leslie; Carol Burnett's daughters Jodie and Carrie Hamilton; and a host of the children of studio executives and producers.

In one of the great ironies of my life, the next year, St. Michael's created a seventh grade, and so if I had gone into kindergarten at age five instead of age four I would have stayed at St. Michael's for another year. I've always thought that might have made a big difference in the rest of the course of my life.

Although the philosophy at Westlake was to try to build self-esteem and there were lots of great extracurricular activities, the academic pressure was fierce. I watched friends in the seventh grade have anxiety attacks about where they would be going to college. One girl fell on the floor crying once because she got an A minus. I found it a harsh place, and though it was in fact a very fine school, it was horrible for me.

My English teacher the first year, Miss Taylor, was an ex-nun who was obsessed with grammar, and especially sentence diagramming. I had never even heard of sentence diagramming and had no idea how to do it. Meanwhile, all the other kids had done it in the previous grades. After two weeks, I was so lost I couldn't complete her assignments, but I was so anxious about it that I found myself unable to tell anyone. I should have said to my parents, "I can't do this," and I know they would have helped me out, but I was paralyzed. Then came our first diagramming test. When Miss Taylor handed me my test back, she gave me a withering disappointed look and put the test facedown on my desk, which made it obvious to everyone that I had failed. That was my first F, and I was humiliated. I had never been a great student, and some teachers had thought I was lazy because I was so often distracted, but before Westlake, I never got below a C. Failing a course was something I couldn't imagine.

I was rubbed raw from the stress and feelings of failure. Though I wanted to ask my parents to switch me to a different school, I thought that they were keen on me going there and didn't want to disappoint them. At the end of that first year at Westlake when I was studying for a science test with my mom, I first became aware of my detailed memory. It was 1978, and I was twelve years old, suffering through the last weeks of seventh grade. As I started chaining back through the days of the much happier year before at St. Michael's, I startled myself by realizing that I could remember what I'd done on the exact same day the year before, and then all the days before that for about a month. *A year ago today I was getting ready for the class picnic; the next day was the school play; the day after that I went swimming at the beach with my friends . . .* I'm sure if I had asked my parents to transfer me to a different school they would have, but at that age, I was terrified that I would disappoint them.

I'm still acutely sensitive that childhood is a time

when we have little control over our lives. Our parents are in charge of all the biggest factors: where we live, where we go to school, what income bracket we're in. I know I shouldn't feel this way anymore, but I can't help it. I still get upset when I think about how I was forced to leave New Jersey and contend with all the pressures I felt of a new life in LA.

All parents desperately try to understand what's going on in their kids' minds, to make sense out of the often strange logic of a child's reasoning, but no matter how hard an adult tries, a child lives in a childhood world that adults left behind long ago. My memory has made me acutely aware of that disconnect. Parents may have a few memories of those early years that help them relate to the intense emotions their children are going through, but they can't really get inside their kids' heads.

My parents certainly couldn't get inside mine, and I was no easy child to raise. I'm still not an easy child for them, because that tempestuous childhood Jill is still so much a part of me. They've been remarkably loving parents, and as I look back through all the years of turmoil in our lives, I am in awe of their steady support of me. We've had our issues, though, and one of those that has been particularly difficult for me to cope with began to plague me during these same years.

Like so many mothers and daughters, my mom and I developed a complex, intensely close relationship, but one fraught with difficulties. At the core of the tensions between us was the way that, from when I was seven on, she would admonish me about my weight. What seemed like almost constant comments seared into my brain with all of the intensity that I felt about them the moment they were spoken, and they still drive me crazy and color my self-image. My mother and I have fought over this issue my whole life, and if I have particularly self-defining memories, then surely those of my mother saying to me, "Don't eat that, you'll get fat," and "Boys don't like to date fat girls," are crucial among them. To her mind, she was just trying to help me make my way in the world and doing her motherly duty.

When she danced for June Taylor, she had been told to watch her weight; Taylor was a tough taskmaster and insisted that her dancers be remarkably slim. I think because my mom had never taken those reprimands personally—she was a professional performer and that just came with the territory—and also because she had no idea I had such an unusual memory, she didn't understand the effect her comments had, and would continue to have, on me.

In combination with the stress I was feeling about the academic pressure of school, her comments about watching what I was eating started to undermine my self-confidence further, making me feel that I wasn't pretty enough and was unworthy of affection. The great irony is that I wasn't overweight. I wasn't incredibly skinny, but I was thin.

I think my mother's obsession about my weight was inspired by a pediatrician I went to when I was seven. He commented to my mother about my "baby fat," and from then on, she was on the case, putting me on a diet and watching my weight like a hawk. When we got to California, the pediatrician there picked up the mission, and I hated my visits to his office. I felt like they were ganging up on me, and meanwhile I wasn't even at all heavy.

Though I took my mother's comments very much to heart, my way of dealing with her admonitions was to rebel. She wouldn't let me eat any of the snack foods that my friends did, and dessert was totally out of the question. To defy her, I'd go to a neighbor's house and raid the cabinet filled with junk food. Over the years, my rebellions resulted in some horrible incidents, among my most dreaded memories.

One of the worst is from June 16, 1979, when I went on a day trip to Universal Studios with my friends Gregg and Alex. My dad was working at Universal as a producer and had gotten us tickets. We had a wonderful day—three kids enjoying the tour—and I bought myself an ice cream cone. When we came back to my house, we went swimming, and when Alex mentioned to my mom that'd we'd had some ice cream, my mom pulled me out of the pool and screamed at me and hit me in front of everyone. Alex and Gregg were stunned. I was mortified.

Another particularly traumatic memory about these weight battles is from when I was graduating from sixth grade. My family was taking a summer trip to New York, and my mother and the doctor put me on a diet to lose five pounds or I wasn't going to be allowed to go. The doctor weighed me every week. When I gained three ounces, I was so distraught that I wasn't going to be able to go to New York that I had a meltdown in his office.

One of the ways in which my mom would try to induce me not to eat prohibited foods was by saying, like a mantra, *If you eat anything bad, I'm going to die.* For a while, she would say that to me every morning when I left for school. The first time I remember her saying it was in early October 1977, when I was eleven. I was stung by a bee, and because I'm allergic, my hand blew up and itched for days. On October 22, my family and me and my friend Lori were going to a picnic that day, held annually by Carl Reiner at Rancho Park, right across from 20th Century Fox. Later I was going to be staying over at Lori's house, and after the picnic, we went back to my house so I could pack an overnight bag.

Right before I left, my mom said to me, *If you eat anything bad, I'm going to die.* Lori's mom was serving pizza for dinner, a definite "bad food." Looking back on this it's amazing to me that I was so upset, but it's a great example of how irrational kids' minds are. I was seriously worried that if I ate the pizza, my mom might die. I did know that believing that didn't make sense, and I was too embarrassed to tell Lori and her parents, so I went ahead and ate the pizza.

By 10:00 that night my anxieties about whether my mother was going to be okay were so bad that I said I had to go home, making up the excuse that the bee sting was bothering me. When I got home, our family friends Beverly and Danny, who have been so close to my family that I call them my aunt and uncle, were there, and I got into my nightgown and all of us danced in the dining room to oldies records. Beverly and my mom kept saying to me, *Aren't you glad you came home?* Glad? Sure I was glad. I was glad everybody was alive.

The effect of all of my mother's harping on me about my weight, in combination with doing poorly in school, was crushing by the time I got to ninth grade. The stress and emotional trauma from the feelings of failure and self-doubt that coursed through me got more and more intense. Finally, on December 8, 1979, a Saturday morning, I couldn't get out of bed for the first time in my life. I was thirteen years old and overwhelmed. My uncle Norman was visiting from San Diego, and my mom kept asking me to get up and get dressed and come out. I couldn't.

For the next six months, I was in a deep depression. I rarely played with my friends. I couldn't make plans, and I hardly left my room, even on the weekends. I was tormented by a persistent recitation in my mind of my failures and inadequacies. There's a powerful line in a song by country western singer Garth Brooks: "It's four in the morning; I'm lying in bed, a tape of my failures playing inside of my head." It was at this time that I fell into a life-long practice of what I refer to as "Y diagramming" in my mind: if I hadn't done this, then that wouldn't have happened; if I hadn't said this, then . . . , blaming myself for being a failure. This is one of the most debilitating ways in which my memory has affected my life. It has instilled in me an acute, persistent regret over so many of the decisions and events of my life.

I read an interesting article recently about what are referred to as "lost possible selves," again by *New York Times* reporter Benedict Carey. He wrote, "It is partly from studies of lost selves that psychologists have come to a more complete understanding of how regret molds personality." The concept is that as we grow up, we may begin to develop the notion that there is a truer self that we might have been or were meant to be. Carey eloquently describes the mental prison these thoughts may trap people in as "that lonely echo chamber of what should and could be."

The rehearsing of thoughts about failures—wrong paths taken, opportunities missed, bad choices made, how we should have known better—has been found to have a profoundly negative effect on people's well-being. This rehearsing is normally one of a process of rumination. For me, though, it's a matter of how my memory operates. Those failures haunted me at the time, repeating themselves in my mind, and because my memory is so complete, they kept doing so through my adolescence straight through my twenties and thirties. They still do.

By the end of ninth grade, my parents couldn't stand to see me in such pain anymore and decided to send me to our local public high school. Suddenly life changed for me again; the academic pressure was lifted, and for the first time in years, I felt relatively at peace. For whatever reason, though, my memory kept getting stronger and stronger and filling my mind up more and more.

Although I'd become more and more aware that I had a much better memory than most other people by this point, I didn't understand that not everyone had the swirl of memories whirling in their brains that I did. I found it increasingly hard to understand how my friends or family could forget the names of people they met, or who started the argument at dinner, or the exact day the episode of their favorite TV show aired; getting the facts right about some family event, or what my parents had told me became increasingly important to me. No one likes a know-it-all, and my insistence on making corrections became a source of quite a bit of friction with my parents. They had no way of understanding what was happening inside my head, and I had no way to describe it. I did start to shock people with the accuracy of my recall, but the true nature of the difference in my memory wasn't at all clear.

I can't know for sure how the unusual richness and

completeness of my autobiographical memories has shaped my sense of self, and how my self-image might have developed if I'd forgotten more. I do know that the process that usually begins in late adolescence and continues in our twenties of culling our memories and crafting them into a coherent and largely self-enhancing life story seems not to have worked in my mind, or at least not at all well. I've never been able to cull bad memories out, and I don't seem to have had the processing mechanism for rewriting them in my mind either and coming to see them in a new, positive way as life lessons. For me, they are what they were. I recall them as documentary-like facts of my life. I feel that surely one of the results for me has been that I retained such a haunting sense of self-doubt and lack of self-worth in place of the positive life story I should have been shaping.

All of the awkward moments at school, all of the frustrations about math, my mother's nagging comments to watch my weight and about how boys didn't want to go out with fat girls, have come to dominate my life, investing me with an intense feeling of being a failure that I struggle with every day. Perhaps the only redeeming aspect of the haunting completeness of my memory for childhood is that I have such a deep empathy for the children I work with and the emotional intensity of their lives.

In a wonderful irony, after having hated school so much myself, I am now the administrator of a school, with kids from kindergarten through seventh grade joyfully ensconced in the middle of all of the heyday of their tempestuous lives. When they come in with their skinned knees or are terrified because their parents are late to pick them up, I feel intensely how real the trauma they are feeling is, and I think they sense that about me.

This past fall, one of the girls at the school came into my office, and I could see that though she was trying to hide it, she was very upset. She told me that her mother had not arrived yet, and when her mom didn't answer when she called her on her cell phone, she was on the verge of panic. She is eight years old, and I knew all too well the terror she was feeling. When her mom appeared at the door a little bit later, she ran to her and blurted out, "I thought you were dead." Because I remember that time of life so well, I knew that she really did fear that her mother was dead, and I try every day to bring that awareness into my work with the children.

What a gift, at long last, to be able to make some good out of the way the traumas of my childhood have continued to haunt me.

CHAPTER SIX

An Archaeology of Time

Writing, I think, is not apart from living. Writing is a
kind of double living. The writer experiences everything twice. Once in reality and once in that mirror
which waits always before or behind.
            —Catherine Drinker Bowen, *The Atlantic*,
                                    December 1957

It is necessary to write, if the days are not to slip
emptily by. How else, indeed, to clap the net over
the butterfly of the moment?
            —Vita Sackville-West, *Twelve Days*

One of the intriguing thoughts in Benedict
Carey's article about the value of writing down
a life narrative was what he wrote about how the crafting

of life stories doesn't seem to really stop; most people are continually recrafting the story of their lives over time. As one researcher who has worked in this area describes the process, "Adult identity can be understood as an anthology of stories that we constantly edit and from which we extract ever-new meanings. . . . We first create the themes or ideologies of our personal stories during adolescence," and then in adult life "we remember, revise, and add to these stories constantly." One of the pioneers in this area of research, known as narrative psychology, is Dan McAdams, who explains the process of continually deriving new meaning from our life memories this way: "Let's say I'm thinking of going to medical school. That may motivate me to think about my past in ways that answer the question, 'How did I get this interest in becoming a doctor?' I may prioritize certain events. I might remember a conversation that I had when I was 16 with a neighbor who was a physician, and think, 'That was a turning point.' In light of my goals, I'll reconstruct the past."

This whole notion of continuous life story modification especially fascinates me because I seem to have no ability to do so; in truth, I do not have any desire to do so. In fact, to me, any changes of the facts or discrepancies in my memories would be highly disturbing. Intellectually, of course, I can see the value of what Daniel Schacter calls bias in telling ourselves the story of our lives, and my own life story has been terribly disappointing, but nevertheless, emotionally the idea of distortions is upsetting.

I may not have crafted the kind of selective life narrative that most people do, but I have kept voluminous records of my actual life narrative. To my mind, the value and comfort of getting the days and the delineations of the discrete phases of my life down on paper has been knowing that I've done so with both accuracy and precision.

Another of the counterintuitive ways in which my memory seems to have affected me is that I have felt a compulsion to keep journals of all the days of my life. As I got older and my memory moved into high gear, with memories constantly flashing through my mind and beginning to drive me crazy, I found that journaling helped a great deal with keeping the swirl under control. If I didn't write things down, I would get a swimming feeling in my head and would become emotionally overwhelmed.

When people first hear about my journals, they often think that I must have memorized them and that they explain why I have such detailed recall. But the truth is that I rarely look at them, and have never spent much time reading back through them. If you look at the photo of one of them here you'll get some sense of how voluminous they are.

For the single five-year period of January 1987 to December 1991, for example, my journal entries cover 350 double-sided 8½ × 11 inch pages, each side divided into 32 boxes of written text measuring 1.5 × 1 inch and containing roughly 60 to 70 words each. That means each

January 1, 1987
through
December 31, 1991

side contains over 2,100 words, the equivalent of 9 typed manuscript pages per side, so my journals for just those years alone number more than 6,300 "typed" pages. The total number of pages in my journals written during all the years I've kept them is over 50,000.

I don't sit and read through my journals, but I do dip into them now and then because I love to be able to go back and see my notes about all the little things that were going on when I was actually writing them. Many people find this one of the oddest things about the way that my memory has affected me. I know there is a contradiction here and it's always been interesting to me. After all, with my memory, I should be the last person on earth who would need to keep a journal. The truth is I really don't know why I was so compelled to write my journals. All I can really explain is what I found satisfying about keeping them.

I think my journaling is part of the same impulse that compelled me to save so many of the items of my life. The closest I come to understanding it is that writing a note about an event makes it real and forever part of history. Once it's on paper, I own it, like owning my books or records or dolls. When a friend once said to me, "I don't understand. If you have it all in your head, why do you need to write it down?" I told him it's because in some indefinable way, it makes these memories real. For me, it's a physical and emotional reassurance that the event really happened. I can't accept living with just the memory. It has to be tangible—something I can hold on to physically, something I can handle. What feels to me like the most accurate explanation is that to write an event down means it really happened. It's like creating an artifact. Archaeologists don't just describe what they found of ancient civilizations. They bring back statues or pieces of pottery, and we build museums around them. My journals are like artifacts for me. I have the record in my mind, but I still want something I can physically look at and touch.

My journal entries are not reflective; they're not commentaries on my life or a place where I work out my interpretations of my life. They are simple records, and the entries just describe key things that happened in a day. Here, for example, is what I wrote for Friday, February 26, 1993:

> Wake up and hang out and relax. At 9 a.m. watch WWOR *Noon News* (from NJ) and at 9:17 a.m. Pacific Time it was announced that there was a bombing at the World Trade Center—glued to the television all morning—call Mom and tell her what is going on—watch TV all day—sit in the backyard and smoke and think about what happened today—sort of freaking out—leave at 2 p.m. and go to Woodland Hills to the Blue Cross office and sign my new insurance papers—home and hang out and watch TV, relax, eat dinner, talk on the phone, TV—watch *Nightline* about the WTC bombing—sleep.

As you can see, my journal entries show the lack of selectivity or focus on the most important moments of a day that is characteristic of my recall; that entry blends both the horrifying news of the World Trade Center bombing with the most trivial details.

I started journaling on Monday, August 24, 1981. I had met my first boyfriend in April. I was a sophomore, and he was a senior, and when he first flirted with me, I was nervous and a little intimidated. He drove a black Camaro with a T-top glass roof and had curly dark hair, and when I met him, he seemed mysterious, a type I find alluring. We didn't start going out until June, and I was crazy about him and the whole experience of dating.

During that summer, I found myself compelled to write down the details of what we did each day on a wall calendar in my bedroom. This was when I launched into my practice of highly detailed journaling.

I think I was prompted to start this more detailed journal keeping because I knew that our relationship was bound to end before long; summer would end, and he was going to start college, and even though he was going locally, things would be different. I was so happy that summer, and I decided that I'd keep a physical record of every day for the rest of the time he and I spent together.

In fact, I had had a kind of prejournal period, which was preparation for writing the journals themselves. When I was a kid in Manhattan, I watched TV in the living room, and as I watched Walter Cronkite on the nightly news, one of my favorite shows, or *The Dick Cavett Show* (which I thought was called the Dick Carrot Show, because of his red hair), I would sit in front of the TV for hours watching the shows and draw lines like this:

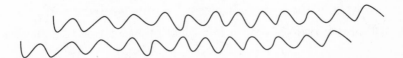

—taking proto-notes before I knew how to write. Years later, in a funny twist, in the summer of 1986, I wound up having breakfast with Dick Cavett at the Beverly Wilshire Hotel. He was a client of my dad at that time. I was tempted to tell him how obsessed with him I had been, but I thought I should probably keep that to myself.

Even before that proto-journaling, I was drawn to record keeping. When we moved to California, I started creating a family tree of our extended family and ancestors on both my mother's and father's sides. I still update it regularly, and the whole family knows that I'm the keeper of our history. When someone has a baby, I add the child, and relatives call to make sure I've done so.

Then, in 1976, when my family went to Phoenix for Christmas vacation with two other families and stayed at the Arizona Biltmore, a vacation I love to remember, I had the urge to make a record of the trip. I was intent not to forget it, and I had the feeling that if I wrote it down, I could keep it with me, like the family tree and the little pocket book full of mementos that I had taken with me from New Jersey. That's when I started writing brief notes on my Girl Scout calendar, which I kept doing year after year, until I got more elaborate with my note making that summer of 1981.

I've stopped journaling several times in my life, but eventually I would realize that I had to go back and get all of that time down. In 1987 I stopped writing in October and didn't start up again until June 1988, when I realized I needed to stop the swirling in my head. It took almost a month, but I got October 1987 through June 1988 down. Then in November 1989 I started my first job, as a production assistant on the NBC sitcom *A Family for Joe,* which starred Robert Mitchum, and I was so busy at work that I couldn't write. When I went on hiatus in May 1990, I again realized I needed to get everything down, and by Friday, June 15, 1990, I had all of 1990 written down in great detail.

In January 1997, I was adamant that I was going to stop: I wanted a break from all of the time it took, and I was determined that was it. I remember telling that to a friend, and he just laughed at me. Too many times my friends had seen me sitting in a corner scribbling notes to myself while everyone else was watching TV or listening to music at parties. Sure enough, that April I was visiting a friend in northern California, and I had brought my daybook with me. As I sat there in the hotel, I started writing everything from January on.

In 2000 I started my longest-running effort to stop; this time it was for four years. But in November 2004 I bought a blank book, divided it into the five years that had passed, and started to write again. By the end of the year I had it all down, and I felt immense relief. I no longer write in my journal most of the time, though, and when I look at my earlier journals now, I am glad that I don't feel as much need to work on them so much. I occasionally decide I want to get back to it, but I'm more selective now about what I cover. After having stopped altogether in 2006, on January 1, 2007, I wrote down all of the special days of the year just passed. I did the same on January 1, 2008, for all of 2007's special days.

I wish I could say that journaling kept enough control over the swirling of my memories that they didn't overwhelm me anymore in the way they had in ninth grade. But when events were emotionally stressful, the memories would get the best of me again. The next particularly bad period after that breakdown in ninth grade, in which my memories raged out of control, was after my boyfriend broke up with me, on December 29, 1981, the day before my sixteenth birthday. We had a good relationship in the beginning, but like most other relationships at that age, the ending was miserable, and it took me a year to get over it. I have a friend who always said, "First loves kill you" and that was the case for me.

What was so devastating was not that I was really so in love with him, but that I kept reliving the relationship. My mind would flash back through the days we'd spent together, and even long after I should have been over him, I'd find myself remembering what we'd done on the same day the year before. We had met on April 1, and when April 1 rolled around, there I was right back in that prior year: *It was two days after President Reagan was shot, and I was hanging out with my friend Dean under the tree near the school's counseling center and Dean introduced me to Harry. . . . And* off my memory went. Then on April 5, I couldn't stop thinking about how, that same day the year before, we had gone shopping together at the Galleria to find a birthday gift for Dean. My memory was stretching the pain of the breakup out beyond all reason; it would do that to me with many of the incidents of my life as I grew older.

Another thing that was intriguing to me about Benedict Carey's article on writing life narratives was that the process can be therapeutic. It apparently can be a way of giving shape to and clarifying learning that's happened in the course of one's life, most often focusing on dramas of achievement, overcoming adversity, learning a major life lesson—stringing together a set of turning points or transformative changes, such as finding your life partner and how that changed you. That's apparently why one's narrative would likely evolve significantly if it was written at several different ages, accounting for changing life circumstances and new achievements, tragedies, and challenges.

Many years ago, psychologists articulated broadbrush descriptions of the shape of the general human life story, most famously Erik Erikson, arguing that each person's life is broken down into a key set of phases, though there is some variation in exactly how many phases are identified and how they are named. One such schema of life's "chapters" is infancy, early childhood, play age, school age, adolescence, young adulthood, maturity, and old age.

These more detailed life narratives that psychologists are now studying are a much more refined, individualized way of understanding the course of our personal development. A leading researcher in this field, Dan McAdams, has shown that a country's culture probably influences the overall type of narrative that people in that country tend to tell, and for Americans, the life narrative is often one of redemption—in other words, of having overcome challenges.

What's so intriguing to me about my experience versus what McAdams describes is that the impetus for me in getting my version of my life story down on paper was different. I found myself naturally drawn to the project of getting a delineation of the main epochs of my life down into an outline, which I refer to as my time line, in order to get the story fixed once and for all. I became almost compulsively fixated on doing so during a particularly stressful period of my post–high school life, and I think that the time line gave me some comfort and helped me feel I had made some sense of my life. I have never shared the time line with anyone before, including the UCI scientists.

It took me quite a bit of doing to get it down right. The notion that I ought to get the whole stretch of my life down this way formulated gradually, and I had been making notes on stickies and scraps of paper for some time and filing them away in a notebook. Then one day I suddenly felt the need to concentrate totally on getting the time line fully worked out, and on Sunday, June 17, 1990, Father's Day, I went to my room and worked on it for almost a full day. I'd get partway through and decide it was off in some way and tear those pages out and begin again. Finally, while watching my new favorite show, *In Living Color*, I had the whole thing down, and I felt an enormous sense of relief and accomplishment.

The list spans my entire life segmented into eras, bookended by significant events. The italicized dates are days that I consider to be life changing—good, bad; it could be either. They are personal anniversaries, and every year I mark these dates when they occur.

You might get a better idea of the way my mind holds on to and sorts through my memories if you tried to break up your life in this way too. Take every significant period of time and date it; break it down into smaller periods of importance bounded by dates; and finally take the specific dates of life-changing events such as births and deaths and great successes and failures and write those in. I bet doing so will be a fascinating experience.

Here is what my time line ended up looking like, though this is an updated version, which I've added to in the years since. The original went only through 1990:

December 30, 1965

January 1966 through March 1971

November 6, 1969

March 1971 through June 1974

    March 1971 through September
        1973

    September 1973 through
        December 1973

    January 1974 through June 1974

July 1974 through July 1975

July 1975

August 1, 1975

August 1975 through August 1977

    August 1975 through August 1976

    September 1976 through August
        1977

August (22) 1977 through June (9)
    1980

    August 1977 through August 1979

    August 1977 through May 1979

    May 1979 through August 1979

    September 1979 through June
        1980

        September 1979 through
            March 1980

        March 1980 through June
            1980

June 1980 through September 1980

September (16) 1980 through June
    (16) 1983

    September 1980 through
        December 1981

    September 1980 through
        March 1981

March 3, 1981

    March 1981 through December
        1981

    March 1981 through June 1981

    June 1981 through September
        1981

    September 1981 through
        December 1981

January 1982 through June 1983

    January 1982 through July 1982

    January 1982 through April
        1982

    April 1982 through July 1982

    July 1982 through September 1982

    September 1982 through March
        1983

    April 1983 through June 1983

June 1983 through August 1983

August (6) 1983 through August (12)
    1989

    August 1983 through July 1984

    July 1984 through January 1987

July 1985 through March 1985

March 14, 1985

  March (14) 1985 through Sept (11)
1985

  September 1985 through January
1987

  September 1985 through
March 1986

  April 1986 through August
1986

  September 1986 through
January 1987

September 4, 1986

  January (12) 1987 through August
(12) 1989

  January 1987 through April
1987

  April 1987 through July 1987

July 8, 1987

  July (8) 1987 through January (5)
1988

January 5, 1988

  January 1988 through January
1989

  January 1988 through May
1988

  May 1988 through October
1988

October 1988 through
December 1988

January 1, 1989

  January 1989 through August 1989

August 13, 1989

August (14) 1989 through May (14)
1990

May 15, 1990

May 1990 through May 1991

  May 1990 through November 1990

  December 1990

  January 1991 through May 1991

June 1991 through September 1993

  June 1991 through September 1991

  September 1991 through March
1992

  April 1992 through October 1992

  October 1992 through February
1993

  March 1993 through September
1993

    March 1993 through June 1993

    June 1993 through September
1993

September 5, 1993

September 1993 through May 2000

  September 1993 through March
1994

September 1993 through
December 1993
December 1993 through March
1994
February 25, 1994
April 1994 through October 1994
April 1994 through July 1994
July 1994 through October
1994
October 29, 1994
November 1994 through July 1996
November 1994 through June
1995
July 1995 through July 1996
July 1996 through December 1996
January 1997 through October
1997
October 21, 1997
October 1997 through May 1998
January 18, 1998
June 1998 through September
1998
September (14) 1998 through May
(14) 1999
May 14, 1999 through May 18, 1999
May 1999 through May 2000
May 24, 2000
June 2000 through December 2001

June 2000 through September
2000
October 2000 through May 2001
June 2001 through December 2001
June 2001 through September
2001
September 2001 through
December 2001
January 2002 through October 2002
October 23, 2002
October 2002 through April 2005
October 2002 through April 2003
December 31, 2002
March 1, 2003
April 2003 through July 2003
July 9, 2003
July 2003 through October 2003
November 2003 through March
2005
November 2003 through
September 2004
September 2004 through
March 2005
March 25, 2005 through April 3, 2005
April 2005 through December 2005
April 2005 through July 2005
August 2005 through December
2005

An Archaeology of Time

This is my version of the story of my life, I suppose. In crafting it, I did identify what I considered to be pivotal events and stages of experience. For example, one entry, *September 1980 through March 1981*, was the first six months of high school, when I had just escaped from Westlake, the school I hated, and I was loving every minute of those months. Another, *April 1983 through June 1983*, covers the three months leading up to high school graduation, a period during which I was thinking a good deal about how much I had grown up.

Working out the phases of my life with such precision was comforting to me, perhaps in a way that is similar to the normal, more selective process of shaping one's life story. But none of these "archaeological" exercises of getting my life down on paper helped me to privilege any of my memories over others, or to distort them in any way, and though some stretches of the time line delineate periods of happiness and of growth, others bracket periods of turmoil and depression.

Rather than using my memories to craft and then recraft the story of my life into a narrative, or as Dan McAdams puts it, into a personal myth, my mind has been intent on fixing all of them, exactly as they happened, in stone. As one article describing the work in narrative psychology explained the mythologizing process: "New work by psychological researchers shows that in telling their life stories, people invent a personal myth, a tale that, like the myths of old, explains the meaning and goals of their

143

lives." By contrast, I would say, my mind has simply told and retold itself the story of the days of my life, day after day, just as they happened. That's not to say that I haven't derived meaning and lessons out of my experiences; I have. I knew that I had grown a great deal through the course of high school, and in those last few months I reflected on that personal growth a great deal. But I also remembered myself as the kid who hadn't grown up yet a great deal, and I think that undercut any ability to make any kind of myth for myself.

McAdams explains that "a life story is a personal myth" that helps to guide people toward the future with a sense of purpose. The fact that I didn't really seem to craft that myth is the reason I struggled so much with heading into the future after high school. I wasn't looking forward to college at the end of high school at all. Just the opposite. The more pressure I felt to move on and start a new life, the more emphatically I clung to my past because, I think, the future for me was all about a continuation of the past.

CHAPTER SEVEN

Speaking Memories

Listening is a magnetic and strange thing, a creative
force. The friends who listen to us are the ones we
move toward. When we are listened to, it creates us,
makes us unfold and expand.

—Karl Menninger

Deep listening is miraculous for both listener and
speaker. When someone receives us with open-
hearted, non-judging, intensely interested listening,
our spirits expand.

—Sue Patton Thoele

Although selecting out positive memories wasn't
something my mind helped me do, another of
the processes that research shows helps us to come to
terms with our memories does seem to work well for

me: the process of talking about them, or more precisely of sharing them with others.

During my twenties, as the grip of my memory became a stranglehold on my life, day-to-day living became a harder and harder struggle. These are extremely difficult years for me to travel back to. One of the reasons that this was true is probably that I had mostly stopped talking about how oppressive my memories had become. It was so hard to describe what was going on in my head and so frustrating—often enraging—when my parents and friends didn't understand, that I pretty much gave up. Everyone in my life knew by this point that I had a remarkably strong memory. I'd share particular memories with them all the time, and fill in dates and remind them of times they'd forgotten as a matter of course. But what I didn't share very much after a point was how horrible it was to live with my memory. If I did try to explain how my memories were driving me crazy, people would usually respond, "Oh, but it's such a gift you have." I couldn't manage to describe what was going on in my head well enough, and they weren't experts on memory and how it affects our lives. How could they have understood?

According to research showing the value of sharing the significant events of our lives with others through storytelling, I think this inability to explain how my memory was affecting me was itself an exacerbating factor in my memories dragging me down. The way that my memories had started rampaging out of control was the most significant happening in my life, and yet I could never truly find a way to describe it effectively, so I could never craft a meaningful story about it for my family and friends. Instead, I went increasingly interior with the torment of it, and I felt horribly alone in my mind.

One area of research about how the storytelling we do about our memories shapes our lives that is especially thought provoking for me has to do with the ways in which memories are shared within families. As one article explained, "This work has revealed different roles in group remembering, such as the narrator (who speaks the most and contributes the most detail to the group recollection), the mentor (who facilitates remembering), and the monitor (who interjects to prevent perceived inaccuracies and to ensure that important details are not left out). Mentors and monitors might be conceived of as listeners who exert clear influence over the group's final recollection." It's fascinating to think about this description of the process versus the way it worked—or I should say, didn't really work—for my family, because I was a dominating player in the game. My family was rocked by a set of traumas during my twenties that had the effect of almost totally incapacitating me. Finally, we went to family therapy, and I was an unrelenting monitor, which totally undermined the purpose. That was all the more unfair because I had caused all of them a good deal of extra stress in those years.

The good thing about that set of family therapy sessions was that they led me ultimately to a therapist who let me talk and talk and talk about the host of memories that were repeating themselves so oppressively in my mind at that time, and the process of talking so much about them accomplished a good deal of healing. I went to one therapist before this one, but none of that therapy had helped me much. The style of my sessions with this therapist, in which I would talk and cry about all of my memories, seemed to be just what I didn't know I'd been waiting for.

This set of "terrible twenties" years really started for me with the issue of going to college. I absolutely dreaded the idea. Once again, I was thrown into turmoil about leaving home. I'd never really liked the idea of going away to college, but I'd always known that my parents were determined that I should go. They thought education was hugely important in life, and there was just no question for them but that I was going. My dad also felt that going to college had turned his life around, and he thought it would do the same for me.

All I really wanted to do at this point in my life, though, was to get a job in LA, ideally working in the entertainment industry, which I knew so much about and had great entrée to because of my father, and then to get married and start a family. My dad found it hard to believe that I wasn't dying to go away to school, but I didn't feel that way at all. Friends have told me how relieved they were to be able to get away from high school and start a new life at college, or were just eager to move on by that point. I never had any desire whatsoever to go to college, and the way I interpreted all of the pressure to go to school was that it wasn't good enough just to be me. All the pressure made me upset that my parents couldn't accept me just as I was.

Eventually I did complete my applications, and I left for college by plane at 2:00 P.M. on Saturday, August 6, 1983. I was seventeen and woefully unprepared. I had such intense separation anxiety that I returned home six times the first semester. Every month I'd be knocking on the door, and my parents were beside themselves. I had a $750 phone bill from calls home to friends. In my mind, my college experience was broken up into three distinct parts, ending up with a sum total of six years and one week of time there from start to finish.

When I was actually on campus, I went wild. I lived in a huge high-rise coed dorm, and there were parties all the time. I met people from all over the country, especially the Midwest and Chicago, and got to know a girl who had grown up in Saudi Arabia. I had fun, and I enjoyed getting to know so many new people. But I really wanted to be home. I kept my emotional distance from my new life, never really committing fully to it. Just when I should have been going through the process of separation from my immediate family, I was instead being pulled back home by my memory.

When I began to do less well in my classes than I had

hoped, memories of Westlake and how I'd felt like such a failure there began to play relentlessly in my head. Once again I felt thrown by academic pressure. Every time I saw the disappointment on the faces of my professors, my mind would flash to the vision of me sitting at home struggling with school assignments that made no sense to me. I tried to fight the memories off by calling up the good times at St. Michael's in sixth grade, but I couldn't beat back the relentless replaying of the bad times.

On top of that, I put on weight, as so many people do when they go to college, and when I went home, my mother harped about that. All the memories through the years of her nagging me about my weight were triggered, and they began to haunt me again relentlessly. Maybe that should have made me thrilled about being off on my own, but I felt nothing like that.

By the end of that first year, I wanted to go home for the summer, but because during the last semester I had contracted pleurisy, a lung disease, and had to take incompletes, I had to stay for summer school. When I finally did get back home on July 7, I was determined not to go back, and for some time I didn't.

In the fall of 1984, I started classes at the local community college, and being back at home allowed me to calm down and find some emotional equilibrium. By the fall of 1985, when I had been home for a year, I dropped all the weight I had gained and began to feel a little better about myself. I seemed to have reached a sort of balance again. My memories were still incredibly insistent, but I was feeling better about myself and learning to come to terms better with the phenomenon in my head. That relative peace didn't last long, though.

On Thursday, March 14, 1985, my dad came home and told us he was going back to the William Morris Agency. The first thing I said to him was, "The Beverly Hills office, right?" He looked at me in anticipation of the storm he knew would come and said, "No, they want me to head the television department in New York." I was shocked. If he had been summoned back to New York in the first years after we had moved to California, I would have been overjoyed. But at this point, the news was devastating.

The fear of leaving and the anxiety of starting all over again overwhelmed me. It didn't matter that I was nearly twenty years old. The feeling that all of my memories from our years in LA would be ripped away was more than I could bear. I was thrown into such turmoil that in July, my parents decided that rather than moving the whole family right away, they would wait until Michael graduated from high school in 1987. For the next two years, my father would commute back and forth, and then we would all move. Among other factors, they had decided to live apart so I would have time to come to terms with the move. Though I wish I could say that I had convinced them not to do so, that I had overcome my anxieties and agreed to go, in truth I was hugely relieved.

I desperately wish I had been able to grapple with my memory and win the fight to let go, but it was no contest. I accepted their decision gratefully.

For that year, my dad lived in New York and came back to California one week a month. My mom flew back and forth often. The stress on them and on my brother was terrible. My brother, who had always been stable and responsible, began to be rebellious and difficult. He would go off with friends and lie to my parents about where he had been, and he started rebelling in other ways too.

Finally the strain was too much for my parents, and in the summer of 1986 they told us that by the end of the summer or early fall, we were moving to New York. On July 29, 1986, I went to New York with the purpose of going down to Washington, D.C., to explore the possibility of transferring to American University. I was emotionally exhausted from worrying about the move and about all of the problems that I was causing my family, feeling guilty and ashamed that I was unable to get over my fears.

I was forcing them to choose between my desperate need to stay, which neither they nor I really understood, and the happiness of the rest of the family. After months of the stress, I was so distraught and conflicted that when I was sent back to California after the trip, I found myself hoping the plane would crash because I couldn't stand the intensity of the situation anymore. As a month passed,

I resigned myself to the fact that we were moving to New York. However, fortunately just then there was a shake-up in the William Morris Beverly Hills office, and they needed my dad back in California. On September 4, 1986, he called me and said, "I'm coming home. We're not going to move to New York." What enormous relief I felt.

Secure in the knowledge that my family was in LA to stay, I suddenly found myself able, even somewhat eager, to return to college. I had found emotional equilibrium again. The day I left to go back to college, January 12, 1987, was one of the few times in my life that I felt I was starting with a clean slate and felt good about that. I believed that everything bad was behind me, all wrapped up. I'd gone through the trauma of almost moving, and it had worked out that my family was staying and my life wasn't going to be disrupted. In addition, my parents had agreed that I could bring my car to college, and I was getting an apartment, so I was confident that the school experience was going to be much better. I could never have anticipated the family crisis that came next—this time a life-or-death battle that taught me a great deal about just how transient our lives are, no matter how firm a grip of memory we have over them.

One of my real regrets in life is that my mother and I fought so much when I was growing up. She had been extremely close to her own mother, and they had a mutually supportive, symbiotic relationship. In fact, the morning after my parents got married, my grandmother, whom I always called Nana, and her sister, Elsie, showed up at my parents' hotel room with shopping bags filled with deli food. My mother didn't think anything of it, and my father knew from that day on that he'd have to make room for Nana in our lives too. Though my mother and I have also been extremely close, the way my mother harped on me about my weight meant that I didn't feel the same kind of unconditional support she and her mother had felt for one another. By this time, the slightest comment from her that I took to be critical would send me into a rage, and we'd have a horrible fight. That's just what happened during Passover 1987.

On Friday, April 10, I came home from college for the holiday. I had contracted an eye infection that was so severe I couldn't open my eyes and had to be walked onto the airplane. On Saturday, my dad almost had to carry me to the doctor. That was the least of my worries that holiday, though.

Monday night, April 13, 1987, was the first night of Passover. My grandparents, my parents, my brother, and I were leaving to head to our family friends' Beverly and Danny's house when an argument broke out between me and my mom. Everyone left while my mother and I got into a terrible fight, and she stunned me into silence when, all of a sudden, she blurted out, "You know, I just want you to know that I went to the doctor, and I'm very sick, and my carotid artery could explode at any time. So keep it up. Keep screaming and making things worse, so it could maybe make my neck explode."

Anger can change to regret in a split second and that was what happened. I stood there in the kitchen horrified as she explained that the doctors didn't know exactly what was wrong. It turned out that her health problems had nothing to do with her carotid artery, but she was under a great deal of emotional stress and people say crazy things in those situations. At least she had gotten my full attention. The news of her illness came out of nowhere. My parents hadn't wanted to upset me, so I had heard and seen no clues. All of a sudden, wham! Everything just stopped. I stopped. My mom stopped. The fight stopped. And as I recall that moment, time stopped.

The next day my mom and I went shopping. Everything seemed normal, but it wasn't. There was a quiet space in my head where even the normal seemed distant, as if seen from a far place where it's clear but isn't. This was the first time that I started to feel what I can best describe as a disconnect from everyday life, which persisted for the next twenty months. I felt strangely distanced from the world and even from myself. It's terribly difficult to describe, and all I can really say is that it was disconcerting.

I went back to college on Wednesday, April 15, though I desperately wanted to stay home. Trying to concentrate on my course work became a nightmare. My mind started racing with memories of times I'd spent with my mother, cycling through our good times and our fights. I called home constantly and came home one more time for a long weekend, April 24–27, but it wasn't until April 29 that my dad called to tell me what the doctors had discovered.

My mother had been diagnosed with tinnitus, a continual ringing or roaring noise in the ear, caused by damage to the hair cells of the inner ear. The actor Tony Randall was afflicted with the disease and created the Tinnitus Foundation to help cure it. What a relief to find that although it was a serious condition, it was not life threatening.

That kind of scare usually sparks introspection, forcing reflection on the relationship that was in jeopardy and how much that person means to you. I should have taken a long look at my relationship with my mother at that point, buoyed by the relief that she was not in danger after all. Perhaps that could have taken place if there was more time. Maybe if it had all ended there, I would have found the inner space to self-reflect. It would have been a perfect opportunity to reconcile our differences and for me to work on our relationship.

Unfortunately, the drama of my mother's condition wasn't over yet. A few weeks later, in mid-May, I came home for two weeks and was waiting to go back for summer session in June. On Friday, May 22, Memorial Day weekend, I walked out the door at 12:30 P.M. to meet my friend Jonathan for lunch. My parents were walking up the driveway as I came out, and my mother was crying in great heaving sobs. I had never seen her cry like that before. My dad looked at me, shook his head, and shooed me away.

Obviously something truly horrible had happened, but I knew my father didn't want to talk to me about it right then. He wanted to be alone with my mother. As soon as I got back home, I found my father, and he told me that my mother had gone for a brain scan that morning. The doctor who had diagnosed the tinnitus thought she should undergo tests to determine the cause of the ringing. The scan had revealed that she had a brain tumor and needed an immediate operation to remove it.

My father saw that I was about to break down from the news and wouldn't tell me anything more about it. For the rest of that day, and in the days following, my parents acted as though nothing was unusual. That very afternoon, my mother was on the phone planning a Memorial Day party. On top of that she invited Danny and Beverly to come over that night so that Danny could help my dad build a new barbecue. I could not join in their stoicism; I was terrified, and my memory went into overdrive, calling up every unkind word I had ever said to her, every fight we'd had through so many years.

When I went back to college for summer school seven days later, I had a migraine headache every day. The summer heat was blazing hot, and I felt weak, so my mom called my doctor and explained what I was going through, and he told her my electrolytes were being depleted. He said to drink Gatorade and take better care of myself. I was constantly worried and nervous. School became a nightmare again because I couldn't concentrate on anything except memories of my mother—good ones that made me angry at the unfairness of her condition, bad ones that made me feel guilty and ashamed.

Every time I called home, the answer was the same: everything is going to be okay. Don't worry. Everything is going to be fine. I was certain that wasn't true, and after a while I couldn't stand being away. The surgery was scheduled for July 8, and I came home on July 2 for the holiday weekend. What did we talk about over that weekend? We talked about the new car that they were getting me. We talked about a party we were having that weekend. We talked about everything but the surgery. The amazing thing to me was that acting as though everything was fine worked for the others in my family. I really didn't understand that then, because I didn't have that ability, and their insistence on not talking about the surgery made me angry.

I was distraught when I went back for the second session of summer school on July 5. On Wednesday, July 8, my mom had her surgery, and I called my dad's office as soon as I got back from class. His assistant was evasive, and that terrified me. When my dad finally called me later, I could tell something had gone wrong. He was always strong and sure, but in that call, he sounded more stressed than I had ever heard him: "Jill, something happened to Mommy's heart and they had to stop the surgery, but don't worry, everything is okay." *Everything is okay.* God, how I hated that mantra.

That was all my dad would tell me, and it wasn't for two days that I found out from my mom's oldest brother that the doctors had to stop the surgery because she had a heart attack during the operation. She had an allergic reaction to the anesthesia and had flatlined. The doctors had to break her ribs in order to get to her heart and shocked her seven times with the paddles before it started pumping again. When I talked to my father about it, he told me that when the doctors came out from the operating room, they looked as if they'd run a marathon. She suffered such trauma that they were going to have to wait to reschedule the operation until she recovered.

That night a strange new feeling began to come over me that added to my disconnectedness and persisted for months. I felt as if I were standing on a ledge, about to fall. It was hazy and indistinct at first, and I don't even know how to explain it fully. Solid ground was gone. I didn't feel that I could step back. I was just stuck on a ledge before some dimly lit huge abyss. The following weekend, I went home.

Finally, we got the word that my mother could have the surgery in November. My parents came out to college to visit on October 9, and I kept thinking that it might be the last time I would see my mom. I wanted to make up to her for all of the difficulties through the years, but as any-one knows who has gone through this sort of experience, there's really no way to do that, at least not in a few days' time. Our parents probably don't really expect us to make amends for all of the hard times raising us; most often they don't even really blame us for all the times we burst into a rage at them, or stormed out of rooms, or gave them the silent treatment. My mind was racing, though, with memories of how horrible I'd been to my mother; scenes of fights we'd had flicked through my mind relentlessly, and I was so on edge that of all things, I ended up getting into a fight with my parents.

I was determined after that to do something to show my parents how much I cared, so I went home a couple of weeks later to surprise them. I will never forget my dad's reaction when he opened the door: he was unhappy to see me. He tried to hide it, and the look just flickered across his face, gone almost as soon as it was there. But I saw it. I felt my whole body react with shock, as if I had just taken a bullet. He just didn't want me there.

My family was, and is, my center. No matter what I had ever done, I knew they loved me and had always for-given me. I had never seen that look before, and now I would live with it all of my life. The pain I gave them is the pain I have to live with too. Forgetting and forgiving are bound so tightly together that one cannot exist without the other. The expression on my dad's face that Saturday, October 24, 1987, will never fade in my mind; it cut to the quick, and at that point, my mind became fixated on remembering the cycle of days that had led up to that day.

One date cued another in a vicious circle: Saturday, January 31, 1987—being mean to my mother. Wednesday, April 29, 1987—the "good" diagnosis of tinnitus. Friday, May 22, 1987—seeing my mother crying and being told about her brain tumor. Memorial Day 1987—the barbecue where no one talked about her illness. July 4 weekend—home to another party where no one talked about her illness. Wednesday, July 8, 1987—the operation and my dad's call to tell me my mom was okay. July 10—my uncle telling me my mother had almost died on the table. July 17—coming home to see my mother in the hospital and causing a huge fight with my dad. October 24—my father's face when I came home to surprise them. All those memories churning through my mind once again overwhelmed me. The feeling of disconnection got so strong I parted company with reality in some way I still cannot define. Tangible things weren't important anymore. I was me watching me, and I didn't care what I did or what I felt.

On Friday, November 27, the day after Thanksgiving, my mother told me that her operation had been postponed yet again and was scheduled for Tuesday, January 5, 1988. She told me that although she knew she could die on the table, she was going to take that chance because she wasn't going to have this brain tumor kill her. The surgery was going to deprive her of hearing in that ear because they were going to have to remove the whole ear canal. But she was facing that prospect with remarkable stoicism.

During the Christmas break that year my dad got me a job working as an assistant to Les Moonves, then senior vice president at Lorimar Productions. Before I left for work on Monday, January 4, my mom, our housekeeper, and I stood in the living room crying and saying good-bye. She was leaving for the hospital that day. There was a moment when I looked at my mother and knew I might never see her again, and it kept me holding on to her tightly. I knew that by the time I got home that night, she would be under premedication for surgery. At work that day, I made it through entirely on automatic. It is one of the few times I have absolutely no memory of the specifics of what I did. I couldn't concentrate at all because my memories were racing so wildly through my mind. The next day, when she was in surgery, would clearly be worse, and I told Mr. Moonves that I was going to stay home, which he was wonderfully understanding about.

The day of her surgery, I was so distraught that I didn't go to the hospital with my father to wait. I stayed in bed all morning, terrified. I simply couldn't go. I couldn't forget her surgery the past July, and I knew that the surgery was risky and she might die. I could not bear the thought of facing that news with all of the family and so many of her friends who would be there around me. I felt I needed to be by myself if it happened. I didn't have the words to explain that to her then, and I didn't understand it myself at the time. She and I both struggled for many years to come to terms with how I had behaved.

I now realize that I needed to know she was alive before I could go there. When Vivian, one of her best friends, called me to say she was all right and the tumor had been removed successfully and she wouldn't need any more operations, I could finally let the fear go. That night when I went to the hospital, my mom was still heavily sedated, and I just sat and watched her, feeling shame that I hadn't come earlier—shame that still haunts me regularly.

From the moment my mother was out of surgery, she went on with her life. What did I do? I could not stop remembering the ordeal, and I felt that I was losing my mind. The detachment I'd been feeling was strange and inexplicable, and I still felt disconnected from myself. I had stopped journaling that past October, after the crisis of my mother's first surgery, and now I was compelled to go back to it. I sat down and wrote all eight months of days from October 1987 to May 1988, and then up to the day that I finished, which was Tuesday, June 21, 1988. The job had taken a month, and it helped me get some control over my emotions from the crisis, but it didn't purge the memories, and a deep fear of my own mortality began to plague me.

Then, two years later, the second big crisis that

rocked my family during my twenties commenced. My mother and father were one of those couples everybody assumed would be together through the good and the bad for the rest of their lives. They had fallen in love in a whirlwind and had never looked back. But our home life had become more and more tempestuous, mostly because my mother and I fought so much, but I had never doubted for one second that their marriage was rock solid. My parents themselves almost never fought. Then starting in late 1989, my father started to feel that he needed a break, though he and my mother didn't tell me and my brother for a while that anything was wrong.

Looking back, I realize that my father's fifty-third birthday, Tuesday, November 14, 1989, was a sign of things to come. That night, *The Godfather* was showing on TV, and my dad had said that what he most wanted to do for his birthday was for all of us to stay home to watch it and order pizza. Then that morning, we got the news that my grandmother on my mom's side, Nana, had suffered a heart attack and was rushed to the hospital. She had moved out to LA in 1983 to be near us because she had developed Parkinson's disease and was beginning to fail. At first she lived in our house, but then she moved into a retirement home close by.

That morning, my mom rushed to the hospital to be with her, and we were hugely relieved when they were able to stabilize her. Later that night, we were still planning to watch the movie, but instead, as happened much too often in my house, a fight started. My brother and I got into it first, and then my mom tried to stop us, and we all ended up yelling. And all of a sudden, my father stormed out of the house. He had never done that before.

He may have been affected by the stress of Nana's condition. Though she hadn't been a fan of his at all when my parents started dating, he knew how important she was to my mother, and through the years he'd become devoted to her and she to him. She came with us on all of our family vacations, and she was a vital part of our immediate family. I'm sure he was also feeling the pressure of knowing how upsetting to my mother Nana's condition would be. But later it became clear that the problem was more deeply rooted and that this was just the first clear sign that he wasn't happy at home.

He didn't move out right away, and as I think about it, I realize he may have been staying at home at least in part due to my grandmother's deteriorating condition. Her heart had been stabilized, but her health took a decided turn for the worse, and she declined steadily over the next six months. On Friday, April 27, 1990, she suffered a massive stroke and was in a coma until she died on Thursday, May 10. Five days later, my dad told my mom he didn't want to be married anymore. He still didn't move out, though; that wouldn't be for several more months, and my parents didn't tell my brother and me for some time.

We could see that my mother was feeling really low,

165

which was unsettling to my brother and me because she had always been such a stoic, but we knew that she was devastated by her mother's death. They had been so close, and now she had to go through all of Nana's things, which must have been horribly painful for her. On top of that, my father telling her that he wanted to leave must have been an enormous blow.

On May 19, my mother told me that things were bad between her and my father. I was completely shocked and didn't in fact really believe her. I had noticed that he was tense, but I was sure that due to all of the stress of her grief over Nana's death, she was overdoing the extent of whatever was going on between them. Then things took another twist. After Memorial Day weekend, my mom felt ill and began to worry that she had symptoms of a brain tumor again. She called her doctor, but he couldn't see her for two weeks, and those two weeks were like reliving the drama of her illness and surgery two years before. This time, however, she insisted there was no way she was going to have the surgery. The operation would require the complete removal of her remaining ear canal, leaving her deaf, and she was determined that she was not going to live without being able to hear. Hit by the emotions of everything that had scared her the first time, along with my father saying he was going to leave, I think she felt she didn't have the strength to go through it all again.

Suddenly life had become overwhelming again. Nana

had died. My mother might be dying, and on top of that she was saying that she and my dad were having troubles. This was when I decided that I had to get my personal time line completely down on paper and holed myself up in my room all day doing so. I'm sure that the trauma of all that was going on had a good deal to do with why I became so obsessed with getting that done.

It wasn't an elixir for my family's problems. Although I was hugely relieved when it turned out a while later that my mother's tumor had not come back, things between her and my father didn't improve, and in midsummer—Monday, July 23, to be exact—my father finally told my brother and me that he was going to leave. Though my mother had told me things were bad between them, I was stunned that he was actually leaving, and I was torn between panic and disbelief. On Saturday, August 4, 1990, my father finally did leave—a day I hate to remember. I still had not accepted that my parents were splitting up, and in the end, they didn't, but years would go by before they would be reconciled. In the meantime, he moved into an apartment in the Wilshire Corridor, a strip of Wilshire Boulevard between Westwood and Beverly Hills twenty minutes from our house.

As he explains it now, he had taken care of everybody in his family since he was fourteen years old, and then all of us, and it had just begun to be too much. His business was high pressure. He was the one everybody came to for help professionally and personally. He had been basically on his own since he was fourteen, and now he was almost fifty-four, and he felt he just couldn't do it anymore.

The strange thing was, though, that he still spent a good deal of time with us. For the first six months, our family life stayed remarkably the same. He'd come over every Sunday night, and we'd go out to a restaurant for dinner, and he was over for every holiday that fall. The situation was confusing, and it took years to work itself out.

Not long after my dad moved out, my brother decided to share a house with his girlfriend. I was home from college by this time and had been a production assistant on several TV shows. I was liking the work, and I probably would have started looking for my own place too around this time, except that I did not want to leave my mother alone. My parents' split sent me into a serious, long emotional decline, with memories of all of our family fights careening through my mind. I still also had a good deal of pent-up emotion about my mother's brush with death, and I was angry at my dad and angry at myself for causing so much turmoil in the house. When my job as production secretary on a game show pilot ended on Halloween 1990, I stopped working. By the time January 1991 rolled around, I hardly went out of the house at all.

My friends would come over and ask what the matter was with me, but I couldn't shake the cycle of remembering, and I didn't want to talk about it with them. I didn't feel mentally disconnected the way I had during my mother's illness, I think because I was in the warm blanket of the security of my home, but I fell into a deep and unrelenting depression.

For the next two and a half years, I stayed very close to home. I almost constantly remembered every event from my mother's illness to my parents' breakup, and the whirl of incessant memories increasingly exhausted me. I should have been working my way up the ladder in entertainment, going out to trendy restaurants and clubs and looking for the man I'd marry, starting the family I'd dreamed of since I was a little girl. Instead, I couldn't get out of bed. I was still much too tied to my past and failing to move on with my own life.

Everyone else in my family was coping with the changes in our lives much better than I was. I was amazed at how they were just adjusting and making new lives for themselves. My brother was upset that they'd split up, but he was coping well and throwing himself into the early days of what would become a highly successful career as a TV producer. I was hiding out in bed.

The only good thing about my parents' separation was that it was the reason that my family went into much-needed therapy. I got out of the house in these years almost exclusively for the purpose of going to those sessions. The family therapy itself was unproductive and unpleasant. I was fixated on going back to when my mother was sick because I still felt so much emotion from that, and the rest of my family, and the therapist too, wanted to focus on the current problems between my parents. I also couldn't help myself from correcting everyone else about their memory of events, which was diametrically counter to the whole point of everyone sharing their interpretations.

What was good about the family therapy for me, though, was that the therapist recommended that I go to therapy on my own and also recommended a therapist, who turned out to be perfect for me. I hadn't understood that I had been waiting for years to talk to somebody about the bizarre phenomenon of all of my memories swirling in my head, and at this point in particular, I felt a tremendous need to rehearse all of the events from the day my mother discovered she had a brain tumor up to my father telling Michael and me that he was leaving the house. The shock from the fear of my mother dying was still very much in my mind—the look on my mother's face walking up the driveway that day played itself over and over. That would set off a whole string of memories in a vicious cycle, and those were what I now needed to talk into submission.

Most people describe the process of therapy—if it is successful—as a journey they make with their therapist. I can't really describe it that way. My therapist hardly said a word to me; he might make one or two observations or give me a different take on something, but he rarely interrupted my steady stream of remembrance. At first I questioned him about why he wasn't saying more, but over time, I realized that just letting me talk things out was the best thing he could possibly have done for me. As I look back on the process, I think that so much of what I needed was to talk about all of those memories nonstop and without offending anyone.

In a way, those therapy sessions were comparable to my journaling. Once I'd verbalized the memories, somehow I owned them in a new way. But there was another great benefit from those sessions: along the way I realized that I had never really allowed people into my life, not fully; I had never shared with them in any truly revelatory way what was going on in my head. By never having been able to make them understand, I had been unable to make sense myself of how my memory was ruling my life, imprisoning me and holding me back so profoundly from the normal process of emerging into a life of my own.

It took seventeen months of talking to get it all out, and then, for whatever reason it was on that particular day, the morning of Tuesday, October 20, 1992, I woke up and my funk had lifted. There was nothing special about the day. It was an absolutely ordinary, perfectly pleasant October day in southern California. I just didn't feel bad anymore. I called a friend who was living in New York, and we talked for a while. When I got off the phone, I made breakfast and realized that I felt lighter of spirit than I ever had before. That morning was the beginning of the end of my therapy and the start of my return to life. The 1992 holiday season was wonderful.

My therapist had told me back in late August that he

was leaving Los Angeles in January to take a job in North Carolina. I was stunned and worried about finding someone new, but I still had five months. As the date got nearer, he told me that he could give me a referral to a new therapist, but he thought I had come a long way and that if I didn't want to continue, that was okay. I have heard that in therapy, it is the last few minutes of a session that are the most important, because that's when you know that you'd better get out what you came to say or you'll have to wait a week to say it. My last therapy session was the day after President Clinton's first inauguration, on Thursday, January 21, 1993, and in those last minutes, I was sure I was done; I had nothing left to say for a next session. I felt that I was making a fresh start, as was the country.

A few months earlier, the sister of a friend of mine had given birth, and I started to take care of her baby almost daily. She was adorable, and I absolutely loved taking care of her. Spending time with her, taking part in the excitement and joy of a new life embracing the world, was rejuvenating. Although I continued to shy away from romantic relationships, my friends had stayed loyal to me, and I resumed my social life. The release from emotional strain that I learned in those therapy sessions proved a lasting ballast for me.

In the end, many years later, my parents got back together, eight years after my dad had walked out of the house. In March 1998, I went out of town for a friend's wedding, and when I came home, my mom right away told me that my dad wanted me to call him. When I did, he said to me simply, "I'm coming home." All he would say at the time was that he realized that he made a big mistake. I was surprised that after all that time, my mother took him back, but when I asked her how she felt about it, she reminded me that he had never asked for a divorce, and he hadn't kicked her out of the house, or ever refused to pay for anything. In many ways, he had continued to be with us and had shouldered his family responsibilities. I found myself listening to her quiet wisdom with new respect, and I envied her ability to move on from the past.

As much pain as my dad's leaving caused, I realize now that we all needed to grow, and ultimately their breakup helped us do that. In those eight years, we all made progress. I am extremely proud when I consider how much my family has been through, and yet we all made it back together. I might have been unhappy with my personal life because I was now over thirty and unmarried and still did not have the family of my own that I had always wanted, but we loved each other and had a better understanding of each other. Best of all, my parents seemed to have revived the magic in their relationship, and I was both happy and surprised they could have gone through so much and could still share that. What I didn't know yet was that I was about to experience some magic in my own life, which would finally help me to come to better terms with the force of my memory in my life.

CHAPTER EIGHT

A Window Opens

Science is the tool of the Western mind and with it
more doors can be opened than with bare hands.
> —Carl Jung, commentary to
> *The Secret of the Golden Flower*

The brain is wider than the sky
> —Emily Dickinson,
> "The Brain Is Wider Than the Sky"

The first touch of magic in my life was the response
that I received on June 8, 2000, from Dr. James
McGaugh, only ninety minutes after having finally sent
him off my e-mail asking for help. I had realized at last
that I really needed to figure out what was going on with
my memory. The therapist I'd gone to had done me a

world of good, but he had no explanation to offer about the swirling of my memories; I imagine he believed, as my mother had always said, that I just dwelled on my past far too much. But I was sure that I wasn't consciously calling up my memories; they were just too random, too spontaneous, and too insistent. There was something different, and something very strange, going on in my head, and I was ready to come to new terms with the phenomenon in my mind. My memory had been ruling my life, and if there were a way for me to find some solace from the constant assault, I was ready for that.

I come from a long line of strong women, and I wanted to be more like them—to cast away my fears of change, of death, of the future and live with the survival spirit that had allowed them to overcome so many sorrows they'd faced in life. One of my favorite memories is of the time when I realized in a profound way just what a powerful, undaunted group of women I was privileged to be part of. On New Year's Day 1989, my family gathered at my Aunt Ruth's house, the last time we were all to be together. My Grandma Helen, Nana, was there; she had taken care of Michael and me much of the time when we were young. My father's mother, Grandma Rose, and her second husband, whom we called Poppy Al, were there, along with my Aunt Ruth and Uncle Jack, my Great-Aunts Molly, Ann, and Minnie (who was ninety at the time and who lived to be 103), and Minnie's daughter, Florence, and her husband, Sandy. Over the next few years, the older generation began to fail and started to pass away. That day, we all sat around the living room sharing stories, catching up on our lives. Then we moved into the dining room for a big meal and spent more wonderful hours eating and talking, and during the course of that day, I realized in a new way just how much the women of my family meant to me, how much I admired their strength and life wisdom.

These were women who were well into their eighties or nineties; they had buried children and husbands, and had faced God knows how many other challenges in their long lives, and there they were—still keeping their heads up, still laughing, still finding pleasure in life. They imparted a new awareness in me that day about the value of moving on in life, of pushing forward rather than always looking back. I had never been able to do so, but at this point I was finally ready to start down a path of discovery that I hoped might possibly free me from my ever-present past. Having taken the first decisive step, with enormous trepidation, and then to have received Dr McGaugh's answer so quickly was simply thrilling.

I knew nothing about the science of memory and had no idea what to expect from my meeting with him. He and I had talked on the phone briefly on June 12 to pick a date to meet, but he hadn't filled me in about what to expect when I got there. I was so excited about the meeting that I got up really early that morning—Saturday, June 24—and as I drove down to Irvine that day, my mind was racing. I wanted to be sure to describe fully what my experience with my memory had been like, to be sure that he understood what a dominant and strange role it had played in my life. I had decided that I would bring him some of my journals. They always provoked a stunned reaction when I showed them to my friends, and I figured that they would be important for him to know about. I had a terrible time deciding that morning which ones to pack; if left to my own devices, I would have hauled my whole trunk full of them down. But my dad told me not to overwhelm him and just to bring journals for a couple of years. In the end, I brought six years' worth.

When I drove up to the research center, the Center for the Neurobiology of Learning and Memory on the UCI campus, I started to feel nervous. The center was housed in an imposing concrete building among a complex of buildings, and I felt completely out of my element. I never had a flair for science in school and had never spent any time with scientists, and the building alone was intimidating.

Dr. McGaugh's office was just what I had envisioned, with an impressive wall of framed diplomas and awards and lined with books. There were books everywhere around the room, with sheets of paper sticking out of them, and whole bookshelves loaded with bound volumes of scientific papers.

After he gave me the tests of dates and events from *The 20th Century Day by Day*, I showed him my journals, and he was clearly intrigued. As he flipped through them, I was anxious. No one had ever read my journals; some of my friends had seen me writing in them, but I'd never allowed anyone to start reading them. I was determined, though, that with Dr. McGaugh, I was going to open up and tell him whatever he needed to know about my memory and my life in order to figure out what was happening in my head. At that point, I was still hoping that he would recognize right away what the reason was that my memory works the way it does.

After we talked for a little while about my life and my experience with my memory, he asked me to lunch, and I told him how the move to California had been so upsetting and after that how I couldn't get thoughts of New Jersey and New York out of my head. At the end of lunch, as we were saying good-bye, he told me that he was going home to "get his little gray cells" to grasp what had just happened. He told me he'd never talked to anyone before who described having a memory like mine and had also never read about a memory like mine in the scientific literature.

The next day, I received an e-mail from him thanking me for coming down and asking if I would come again in July. We set a date of July 8, and that day I met the two other scientists who would participate in the study of me. Dr. McGaugh had contacted them because they had areas of expertise in the study of memory that were complementary to his. He told me that he would like me to undergo a series of tests and explained they would be the beginning of what would likely expand into a longer-term study.

One of the scientists Dr. McGaugh chose to team up with was Dr. Larry Cahill, a neurobiologist, and the other was Dr. Elizabeth Parker, a neuropsychologist. I was quickly to learn that the study of memory is a vast area of science, spreading over many specialty fields, and that even many of the most basic questions, such as just how a memory is formed, how and where our memories are housed in our brains, and how the process of remembering works physically, have yet to be conclusively answered.

Dr. Cahill's area of expertise, neurobiology, is the study of how our neurons form circuits in our brains and how those circuits help us to process information: to perceive, think, feel, and, key to working with me, form and recall memories. Dr. Cahill's special interest has been in how our brains store information, and especially how they sort out which information is important to store and to be able to retrieve, and which is better discarded, or at least stored in a way that mitigates against retrieval. The notion is that all of our brains are crammed full of information but that most people have neural circuits that allow the retrieval of only a selective sliver. One of the big open questions in the science of memory concerns whether our brains may in fact store a record of everything that has happened to us—of every day of our life—

but that our memory retrieval circuits tap into only a tiny portion of that vast storehouse.

On his faculty profile Web page, Dr. Cahill features a fascinating quote from one of the founders of psychology, William James, that resonates powerfully for me: "Selection is the very keel on which our mental ship is built. And in the case of memory its utility is obvious. If we remembered everything, we should on most occasions be as ill off as if we remembered nothing." Dr. Cahill found my memory interesting in part because he has worked on the question of whether it's because memories are particularly emotional that we remember them, and my memory doesn't seem to select for them in that way.

In investigating the processes of memory formation and retrieval, Dr. Cahill has incorporated the rapidly developing techniques of brain mapping into his work, through imaging of the brain with PET scans and fMRIs, which take pictures of the brain during the process of thinking. Eventually that avenue of research into how my memory works was to lead to some astonishing results. It's only recently that I've learned what those scans revealed.

Dr. Parker's area of expertise, neuropsychology, focuses largely on the study of symptoms that are associated with brain disorders or injuries. She has studied athletes who suffered brain injuries, for example, as well as people with amnesia and other cognitive disorders. The work she would do with me would be to administer a series of diagnostic tests to evaluate my memory functioning and my general cognitive abilities.

A great deal has been discovered about the functions of different regions of the brain from the study of people with cognitive impairments and about the interconnections among the brain's regions. One of the most famous of such patients is the man known in the scientific literature as H.M., who has played an important role in the development of neuropsychology. He was epileptic, and in 1953, he elected to have radical brain surgery in an attempt to cure terrible seizures he was experiencing. The surgery divided a section in the middle of the brain that plays a vital role in memory, especially the recall for facts and events, which is called the medial temporal lobe. He has been studied ever since the operation due to its tragic side effect: he developed a severe form of amnesia. Although his memory of his life before the surgery was not impaired, except for the time just preceding the surgery and some of his memories for a decade or so before, he was unable to form certain kinds of new memories.

He is unable to create long-term memories for events, so does not have autobiographical memory for the long stretch of his life that has followed the surgery. This impairment has not stopped him from being able to learn new information, such as a range of tasks that scientists have taught him to test this ability. The complexity of the types of memories he has been able to learn, and of the ways in which his memory is impaired, have provided a treasure trove for study, making enormous contributions to the understanding of how the anatomy of the brain relates to memory functioning.

The field of neuropsychology has evolved rapidly in recent years, and it can provide invaluable clinical assistance for people who suffer brain damage or have a disorder. One of the things I'd like this book to do is to bring the field more into the public's awareness because, as Dr. Parker explained to me, many people never get neuropsychological treatment because they don't even know that they might be able to get help. I know what a comfort it was to me to have verification of the nature of my memory and all its quirky functions, and I can only imagine the difference it would make for so many others who don't even know what they're suffering from.

One of the stories Dr. Parker told me, of a patient who was referred to her, has especially stuck with me. The woman could barely talk; she had aphasia, a condition whereby people's speech is badly impaired because their brains are unable to put words together appropriately. She might say a sentence such as, "I'm going to drink the straw now because I'm tired of the clock." Dr. Parker believed she had damage to an area of a particular part of the brain, which such speech problems are symptomatic of, and it was so sad to me that this woman had been suffering for so long without any idea what was wrong with her.

One of the great challenges in the study of the brain is

that it's difficult to see inside it. We can see a broken bone, or a tumor, or that a wound is getting infected. But tucked away inside our skulls, the brain and its circuits are illusive. Even with brain scanning developing rapidly, so that ever more refined pictures of the brain are possible, those pictures are taken as if from 2,000 feet from the surface of earth. The specific neuronal circuits are so delicate and intricately woven that they don't show up on the scans.

Neuropsychological testing is a vital way to get a more detailed mapping of what areas are damaged and to point to possible therapy or treatment. One of the most profound realizations I've come to through my work with the scientists is that even with all of the amazing developments in brain science over the past couple of decades, the understanding of the brain is still in its infancy. The study of superior memory is an area that's particularly undeveloped.

As Dr. McGaugh explained to me later, the battery of tests to evaluate memory functioning have been designed with the purpose of measuring degrees of impairment, not to measure how much above the norm a person's memory abilities might be. As it would turn out, I would get perfect scores on a number of the tests I took, but those scores weren't able to tell them just how much higher I might have scored if the tests were designed to measure abilities well above the average. The team would therefore not only administer a selection of the standard memory and general cognition tests, but would tailor some additional tests specifically to measure my abilities, for example, tests of my ability to recall the days of the week for dates they randomly selected, as well as of my ability to recall current facts about events, and my recall of autobiographical events. They would also interview me to get a life history.

I had several sessions with Dr. Parker, starting on July 15, in which she conducted the life history interview. It was like another round of talk therapy. Then she administered a battery of standardized neurological tests. These are used to evaluate strengths and weaknesses in people's brain functioning, including a group of memory tests known as the Wechsler Memory Scale–Revised (WMS–R), an updated version of a set of tests for memory devised in 1945 by pioneering American psychologist David Wechsler. The WMS–R measures memory abilities in areas such as auditory recall, visual memory, immediate recall, and working memory, as well as what is referred to as general memory. My test results were to reveal an atypical pattern: Generally people score at about the same level on most of the tests. But my results showed that my memory was extremely strong—very far above the norm—in some areas and yet relatively weak in other areas, which, as Dr. Parker was to explain to me later, was verification of what I had told them about how much difficulty I had with memorizing generally and especially when I was in school.

Dr. Parker was warm and clearly sensitive; she came across as a deeply caring person, and I felt comfortable with her right away. She could not inform me, at that point, about what each of the tests was designed to measure, as that might affect my performance. Some of them were strange to take; some were a breeze and fun, whereas others boggled my mind. I was asked to recall lists of words I'd read, and also to recite back to her, in reverse order, strings of numbers that she read out to me. A frustrating one was the Stroop Color and Word Test, in which the word for a color appears on a computer screen but in a different color from the word. So the word *blue* might appear in yellow and the word *green* might appear in red. I had to choose from the four color words at the bottom of the screen which one was shown above. The test measures how fast a person's brain gets past the fact that the color and the word don't match and allows the person to choose the correct color name.

A much more enjoyable test for me was the Proverbs Test, in which the assignment is to write the meanings of a set of twelve widely known sayings, such as "A tree is known by the fruit it bears," "Don't cross bridges until you get to them," and "The harder the storm, the sooner it's over."

Although the purposes of these tests were mystifying to me, I was hopeful that all of the testing would produce some answers, and I felt relieved to be involved in a truly scientific process of discovery about my memory.

Over time as I met with the scientists, they would spontaneously quiz me about dates, and later each of them would tell me that there was a special "blown-away" moment when he or she suddenly understood just how different my recall abilities are. For Dr. McGaugh that moment was on the first day I met him, when I corrected the date for the taking of the hostages in the U.S. embassy in Iran from November 5 to November 4. For Dr. Parker that moment was when I got a perfect score on the facial perception test. She told me later that was when she knew she was dealing with a mind that was substantially different from any other one she'd studied.

For Dr. Cahill, the aha! moment was when he brought in an article about the *Murphy Brown* TV show's Christmas episode in 1988, the first year of the show, and quizzed me about the date it was broadcast. I immediately told him the date was December 11, and he shook his head, disappointed, and told me it had aired on December 18. I shot right back that I was sure that was wrong, because on that day, I was watching *The Brady Bunch* Christmas movie at home, which was on the same network in the same time slot. He looked stunned that I would remember that. To prove to him that I remembered right, when I got home, I dug out my TV episode guide book and confirmed that in fact the episode had aired on December 11 and I faxed him a copy of the page. Over the years I would report to him about lots of dates I had found in books or magazines that were wrong, faxing them to him that way.

In early 2001 the scientists called to tell me they wanted to fill me in about the results. I went down to Irvine to meet with them on Saturday, February 24, 2001. Dr. Parker had written me a letter summarizing the results, and reading that letter was a watershed moment in my life:

> *Dear Jill:*
>
> *I wanted to provide you with a summary of your test scores after undergoing neuropsychological testing with me. . . . In my opinion, the test results provide a valid estimate of some areas of your memory and cognitive functions.*
>
> *I administered the Wechsler Memory Scale, Revised, and it indeed shows that you have a very superior memory. . . . What this particular test indicates is that you have good memory in both visual and verbal domains. . . . In addition, you have remarkable attention and concentration abilities. . . . Certainly your ability to work with information in mind is indeed remarkable and tests out very high.*
>
> *Your superior memory, which has been and is the area of concern that brought you to see us, is documented on a number of the tests. . . .*

I think perhaps the most powerful words were those that confirmed that my sensation of my mind processing information differently, and the workings of my memory being so unusual, had been confirmed:

> *The variability in your test scores is entirely consistent with your sense that you have cognitive abilities that do not fit the average pattern. . . . There are certain areas of memory that are consistent with what you said in terms of your difficulties in school when it came to rote memorization. Thus, I think your neuropsychological test results are quite consistent with your own report of the paradoxical fact that despite having excellent memory, there were certain areas of your academic and scholastic training that presented some difficulties. You mentioned having trouble learning rote passages of poetry, for example. . . .*

What an amazing feeling it was to be getting scientific confirmation about the phenomenon that I'd never been able to describe to my family and friends. There was clearly a long way to go yet before we would know what was really going on in my head, but at least I now knew for sure that I wasn't crazy.

The scientists explained that this set of results was just the beginning of the process. For one thing, none of the tests I had taken yet had been designed to test for the automatic nature of my recall, and they were going to devise additional tests to assess that. For example, one of the tests they eventually gave me, on Friday, November 21, 2003, was to ask me, with no warning, to write down the dates of all of the Easters that I could remember. I started in 1980, the first year of my strong recall, and within 10 minutes, I wrote down all of the dates and also short notes about what I had been doing on those days. The list was reproduced in the paper the scientists published later as follows (again, some of the descriptions of what I was doing I preferred not be published and so the scientists indicated them as simply "personal"):

AJ'S UNEXPECTED RECALL OF ALL EASTERS SINCE 1980

This list was produced within 10 minutes. There is one error and it is off by two days. We have not found anyone who can find the error without resorting to a printed calendar. Nor have we found anyone who can produce this list of dates.

DATE	PERSONAL ENTRY
April 6, 1980	9th Grade, Easter vacation ends
April 19, 1981	10th Grade, new boyfriend, H
April 11, 1982	11th Grade, grandparents visiting for Passover
April 3, 1983	12th Grade, just had second nose reconstruction

April 22, 1984	freshman at (school), Cs (friend) parents visiting
April 7, 1985	just returned from a week in AZ, sick as a dog
March 30, 1986	parents in Palm Springs, W, G, A (friends) staying at house
April 17, 1987	B (friend) for Easter, vomit up carrots
April 3, 1988	personal
March 26, 1989	Bs (friend) for Easter
April 15, 1990	make cookies, S breaks up with me next day
March 31, 1991	R (friend) visiting, gets carded for cigs
April 19, 1992	Easter dinner at . . . T(friend) comes over
April 11, 1993	hang all day, spaghetti dinner with R
April 3, 1994	wake up at H's house
April 16, 1995	rainy day, brunch with H (friend)
April 7, 1996	personal
March 30, 1997	dinner with J and C (friends)
April 12, 1998	house smells like ham, M (friend) over
April 4, 1999	hang, describes specific event at work
April 23, 2000	Las Vegas for weekend
April 15, 2001	personal
March 31, 2002	hang
April 20, 2003	hang with J (husband) and family

As their note at the top indicates, I had gotten one date wrong by two days. When they asked me to write the list again, spontaneously, two years later, I got all of the dates right, and when they showed me the two versions side by side, I immediately pointed out to them the one error that I had made the first time. They were particularly impressed by my ability to recall these dates because for one thing, the date of Easter varies so much year to year, and also, because I'm Jewish I don't celebrate that holiday.

They informed me that they were applying for approval and funding for a more extensive study and that getting the approvals would take some time. Another component of the additional testing they wanted to do was to make a series of brain scans in order to try to determine if there were any unusual structural features of my brain.

Little did I know how methodically and slowly the wheels of science turn. Many more months would go by before I would hear more from the scientists, but in the meantime, I was to experience the other magical transformation in my life that I could never have expected would come along.

CHAPTER NINE

Beginning Again

The heart that truly loves never forgets.

—Proverbs

Each moment of a happy lover's hour is worth an age of dull and common life.

—Aphra Behn

The word I received from the scientists, confirming that my mind really did work differently from most other people's, was empowering and liberating in a way that is hard for me to describe. I was thrilled at the prospect of finally learning, as their work with me continued, what was really going on in my mind, and in these later years of my thirties, I reached a new balance in coping with my ever-present past. But my life was not at all the way I had dreamed it would be. From when I was a small child, I had imagined that my life would be centered around a wonderfully happy marriage and raising lots of children. By this time, that seemed the prospect of a long-lost life, a life I had simply not been destined to live. Then suddenly I was to fall in love.

The Internet had connected me to Dr. McGaugh, and now it would connect me to another man who would change my life—the warm, strong, confident, and hugely likable man who would become the love of my life, Jim Price.

I had become fascinated with searching the Web a few years back, in 1999, when John F. Kennedy, Jr.'s plane went missing. I was riveted to the television set all week-end, and when I went to work on Monday, July 19, 1999, I got on the Internet at work and kept track of the news. Immediately I was hooked. What I loved most was the way the Web could serve up any kind of news and infor-mation, and I began reading several online newspapers every day and sampling articles from newspapers all over the world. In keeping with my obsession about the past, I especially loved searching the phrase "today in history," and was consumed by reading all about the things all over the world that had happened that day. The next thing I knew I was making notebooks in the same spirit as my journals, and over the years I filled many looseleaf note-books with writings and records.

My surfing took on a new nature when on October 18, 2002, my computer at work was upgraded to a new version of AOL, which made accessing chatrooms a snap. I had never participated in chatrooms before, but I discovered that I loved them. I've always been curious about what was going on in other people's lives; I love to sit in airports or when waiting for friends at a restaurant and watch people or listen to their conversations, and I love getting people to talk about their lives. Surfing around chatrooms was a way of listening into conversations and talking to people all over the world. That's what I did for three straight days: went into AOL chatrooms and dove into the dialogue.

I went into the Jewish room. I went into the Christian room. I was talking to people who were Backstreet Boys fans, and to those chatting about 9/11. I checked out chats on current events and participated in conversations about the most banal things. One day I went into a chatroom and asked who likes tuna sandwiches on rye bread. The next thing I knew, everyone was chatting about their food cravings.

I had pretty much given up on actively looking for love by this point and had come to the conclusion that if it was meant to enter my life, it would just show up, by providence; it wasn't something that I could make happen. Never in a million years when I woke up on the morning of October 23, 2002, would I have thought that I would meet my husband later that day. His name was Jim Price, and in the short time we had together, he gave me the gift of a new life.

I entered a random chatroom in which thirty-six people were logged on and started chatting away with them. Suddenly James22 started talking to me, and before I knew it, everyone had stopped talking and only he and I were writing on the screen. The thirty-six people were still logged into the room but only he and I were chatting. We talked back and forth for a few messages and then, oddly, because we hadn't been writing anything romantic, somebody in the room typed in: *You should try love*, and logged off.

James22 then asked me, *Do you mind if I Instant Message you privately?* It was so surprising that I was almost startled; I hadn't ever gone off-line that way from a chat before, but I was intrigued and decided to take the leap. We popped off and he IM'd me. I found talking with him completely natural.

After a few minutes of easy back and forth covering the basic hellos, he wrote: "So how do I get to know you better as a friend first?" I didn't know how to answer, but I loved that he had asked me that. Being such an archivist of my life, I of course printed out and saved that first chat, and the many others that followed. I didn't know exactly how to answer his question, but he thoughtfully helped me along the way, and before I knew it, we'd agreed to pick up the conversation later that night. It was such a simple conversation, but it came to mean the world to me:

Gyll23: good question

James22: its hard to answer sometimes but id really would like to know more about you

Gyll23: what do you want to know?

James22: anything you feel comfortable sharing with me

Gyll23: lets see . . . I have lived in CA since I was 8; I am from NYC and have a younger brother I work in the entertainment business and my dog's name is Walter.

James22: I've lived in cali all my life. I have two boys.

Gyll23: What are your boys' names?

James22: Ben is 14 Tyler is 11

Gyll23: love the name Ben

James22: yea is very cool name

Gyll23: What grade are they in?

James22: bens in 8. Tyler in 6. Ben goes to high school next year

James22: Are you tall?

Gyll23: 5' 7" how about you?

James22: perfect I'm 6'1

Gyll23: tall!!!!

James22: yea I guess so

Gyll23: when I was in high school I dated a boy who was 6' 5" and he was the shortest brother!!

James22: WOW what color hair do you have?

Gyll23: dirty blonde

James22: very good
Gyll23: And you?
James22: blk and gray and hzl eyes
James22: hey hunny
Gyll23: Yes?
James22: I need to go pick my kids. Will you be
    around so we can talk later?
Gyll23: I leave work at 7 pm talk then
James22: yes we will sweetie

It was that simple. With Jim, right from the start, I had no reservations, no worries about my looks or my weight. We were just two people in the air somewhere in cyberspace. As it turned out, Jim didn't wait until 7:00 to get back in touch. I had AOL up all that day at work, and he checked in with me again several times. I learned that he was thirty-nine, two years older than me, and had been divorced for four years and had two sons. Then I filled him in about my memory, and he was fascinated. He had written about his son Ben, and our conversation flowed from there as follows:

Gyll23: so Ben was born in 1989
James22: yes . . . and Tyler in 91
Gyll23: what date?
James22: sep 20th
Gyll23: I remember where I was that day.
James22: you do?

Gyll23: yes

James22: Where?

Gyll23: He was born on a Friday?

James22: yes he was

James22: 8:10 pm

Gyll23: I have a photographic memory beyond
comprehension

James22: wow very kool

Gyll23: Ben was born on a Wednesday.

James22: yes wow at 1:47 am

Gyll23: I had just returned from Florida the day
before. Am I freaking you out?

James22: no I think its very kool

James22: see im very good with numbers and faces

Gyll23: tell me what year and date you were
married and I can tell you what day it fell on.

James22: June 18 1998

Gyll23: numbers, dates, names, faces . . . drives
me crazy sometimes.

Gyll23: do you mean 1988 . . . if so it was a
Saturday

James22: yea sorry

James22: and what else was that day

Gyll23: the day before father's day . . . my friend
Larry's mom died that day . . .

James22: very impressive

Gyll23: I could blow your mind.

James22: You already have

I had never experienced anything like the easy back and forth I had with him, and I liked him from the first moment. He seemed unaffected and grounded, and when I told him about my memory, he'd found it intriguing. Later he grew even more fascinated by it and would tell people that they should ask me to date some event from their lives, showing my memory off for me. Meeting Jim on the Internet freed me from the inhibitions I would have felt if I had met him first face-to-face. In person, I would have been plagued with self-doubt. How do I look? How do I sound? How quickly should I reveal things about myself? I knew people often lied on the Internet, but Jim felt genuine to me, and the more he and I chatted that day, the more intrigued I became.

Surprising as it was to find myself coming to this conviction, that very day, after just those few chats with Jim, I decided that all the things in my past that had held me back were not going to stop me anymore. I wasn't going to let my fears get in my way. I wasn't going to worry that I would always remember the bad experience this might turn out to be. That was probably the first true moment of spontaneity in my adult life in which my memory was not holding me back. I was not yet in control of my memory, but I believe that in that moment, I began to get out from under its control.

Later that night, Jim and I talked on the phone, for five and a half hours. In our last chat, we had agreed that he'd call me at 10:30 P.M., and as the time got closer, there were more and more butterflies in my stomach. I had printed out the transcripts of all of our chats during the day, and as I sat in my bedroom reading through them, I realized how much I wanted things to work between us. I even practiced how I was going to say hello because he'd never heard my voice.

In a funny way, I did feel a little like I was deceiving him, because the person he spoke to at the beginning was the person who I was always meant to be—not the person who had been so thwarted by her memory—and that's who he was attracted to. But for whatever reason, it was at this particular point in my life, with this utterly unexpected opportunity, I decided that for the first time since I could remember, I was going to proceed as if I had nothing to lose and I was not going to be scared. On the phone that night, I felt that I was somebody totally different from the Jill I always had been. I was the Jill I was always meant to be.

I learned more about how to embrace life from Jim during the time we spent together than I had from anybody else in all my life. We were from almost diametrically opposed backgrounds—different religions, different lifestyles, different socioeconomics. He grew up poor; I grew up with money. I spent my summers on the beach or in the swimming pool in my backyard; Jim was sent to work in a defunct gold mine that his grandparents owned in the Sierra Nevada Mountains. He and his brothers would be shipped up there at the beginning of the summer to stay with their grandparents and work, and the place was so remote that when the sun went down, they had to go to sleep because there was no electricity.

I grew up in Los Angeles, shopping at boutiques, eating in great restaurants, taking extravagant vacations. As Jim put it, he grew up eating government cheese. Even our taste in music was completely different. He loved rock and heavy metal, and I loved almost every kind of music *but* those. He lived for the Ozzfest and was extremely proud of his T-shirt collection from all the years he'd gone. Jim was a seriously casual guy; he wore flannel shirts and swore he'd never wear a three-piece suit because he wasn't that kind of person.

He had basically been on his own from the time he was seventeen years old, and he was married with his first baby before he was twenty-six. He had worked as a machinist and a mechanic, and he knew how to fix cars and make any kind of home repair you might need. My dad and my entire family were helpless that way. Changing a lightbulb in my house was a major construction challenge. For anything beyond that, we called a repairman.

Jim was a wonderful father, deeply devoted to his sons, and he had loved being married, but after seventeen years, he and his wife had drifted apart. Over the past several months before we met, when he wasn't with his kids, his life had become a dull routine. He told me he would come home from work, take a shower, and go to sleep. To my great good fortune, he had decided that it was time for him to meet someone new.

It was exhilarating to feel free and easy and comfortable and relaxed. The feelings I was having were so new that I almost couldn't recognize them for what they were. Friends had always told me that falling in love was that way. I just never had before.

That first night on the phone, Jim and I even watched television together, and for stretches as he watched his screen and I watched mine, we just listened to the sound of each other's breathing. It was as if we were sitting side by side on the couch, a comfortable old married couple. When we finally got off the phone, it was 3:30 in the morning. I got into bed, and my heart was pounding so hard I could hardly breathe.

On the way to work the next morning, all I could think about was whether he'd be on the computer again that day or whether he'd call me. I did talk to him that day, and that night, and we talked Friday night too, after I got home from dinner with a friend, and then again on Saturday and Sunday night.

The next step was for us to meet, and I was scared. He had e-mailed me a picture of himself, but there was no way I was going to send him one of me. What if he hated the way I looked? We might not have met for months because Jim lived up in Napa Valley, north of San Francisco, but it so happened that in mid-November, he was coming down to LA for a friend's wedding. He asked me if I wanted to get together after that, and I agreed. We made plans to meet on Tuesday, November 19, 2002, the most momentous day of my life.

I had reserved a hotel room because I wanted us to have privacy. I had told my mother I was meeting Jim and would be away for the night, and although she was worried because we had met on the Internet, I was thirty-six after all, and I didn't need to ask for her permission. The only thing I wasn't ready for when the day finally came was that Jim showed up early. He called me at the office around 2:00 in the afternoon, and I sent him over to the Century City Mall because I couldn't leave work until 7:00.

We arranged to meet in a park in Beverly Hills, and when I pulled up I saw him sitting in his car right away. Seeing him there was one of the scariest moments of my life, but I made myself pull into the spot right next to him. We got out of our cars at exactly the same time, and he just pulled me into his arms and started kissing me. There was an instant physical attraction between us. After all the days of anticipation, we were finally standing there for real, and there was no awkwardness and no distance. I had never felt that way before, and my defenses weren't just down—they were nonexistent. He said my heart was beating so fast that he could feel it. In his wonderful supportive, caring way, he right away told me he thought I was beautiful and sexy, and I cannot tell you how much those words meant to me. In our time together, he told me that every day.

Jim was a big man, roughly 6 foot 1 inch, and a very well-built 200 pounds with broad shoulders that looked as if he could lift a car. His hair was salt-and-pepper, and he had a thick mustache and hazel eyes. He wore glasses because he had type 1 diabetes, and it had affected his vision. The first thing I made special note of about him that day we met were his hands. I loved those hands. They were strong, with long fingers, and when he talked, he talked with them gracefully. They were exactly what I always thought a man's hands should look like.

I had always thought that my husband would be like my dad, and Jim was completely different. He had five tattoos—on one arm a cougar and on the other a lunar eclipse. Running down one leg, the whole length of his thigh, was a castle, and if you really sat and looked at it, you could see people in the windows. On the other leg was a huge wizard. He also had three earrings—a diamond and two gold hoops.

I let Jim see everything about me, and I don't just mean physically. I mean all the things that we hide from the rest of the world behind our public faces. He was the only person except for my brother and my parents who has ever really fully seen my private face. Even my friends saw only bits and pieces of me. They knew about my memory, but they knew almost nothing about how it had tormented me in my life. Jim saw inside me and saw the years of scars and the pain my memory had caused, and he accepted everything about me. That was an enormous gift.

When we made love for the first time, the second night after we'd met, I felt healthy and utterly uninhibited. I had never known the beauty of a great sexual appetite, or that great love and great sensuality went so well together, and I marveled that I could feel so close to him so quickly. I had never felt anything like that connection with any of the other men I'd dated. At thirty-six, I finally really became a woman.

I think my parents were taken aback about how quickly we'd gotten together. We went to my house for dinner on that first trip of his, and my mom took some pictures of us. I think she may have wanted a photo of Jim in case I disappeared and they had to call the police. Jim would later tell me, "You know every time I touched your hand or moved closer to you, I'd look up at your mom and she was glaring at me." I said, "She was memorizing your face in case you murdered me so she could give a good sketch to the cops."

That first night at the hotel as I lay in his arms, he suddenly looked at me and said, "What are you doing for the next forty years?" And I answered, "I don't know. What are we doing?" He just smiled, and I felt that the entire universe had moved into a new position.

On Friday, December 6, I flew up to Napa to meet Jim's sons and see his world, and though I was nervous about the trip, that weekend was one of the best of my life. The night I got there, I realized that Jim made me feel completely safe. Ever since I was a baby, I had needed some kind of noise to help me get to sleep, whether it was from the Roosevelt Hospital Emergency Room across the street in New York, or the first of many radios in New Jersey starting at the age of six, or the television that was put in my room in March 1983. Even so, I had suffered for fifteen years with insomnia, and for the four years before I met Jim, I had finally been sleeping but with the help of the television. When I got to his apartment I was surprised—and a little worried—to find out he didn't have a television set in his bedroom, and I figured I'd be up all night. But as soon my head hit the pillow I was fast asleep. In Jim's arms I felt safe and secure.

Although I had been speaking to the boys on the phone for a few weeks, I was nervous about meeting them. When I got off the plane, I was so nervous that I stopped in the bathroom to freshen up and collect my thoughts. This was a meeting that could change my life forever. In the arrivals area, Jim was waiting with Ben, the thirteen-year-old, and to my enormous relief, Ben had an excited glow on his face. Both of the boys welcomed me into their lives warmly, and I told myself it was a good thing they were boys. Remembering as vividly as I did what it was like being a teenage girl, I knew that if my father had brought a girlfriend home to meet me at that age, I would have given her the third degree.

Jim's kids meant the world to him, and I was, and am, undyingly grateful that they welcomed me into their lives so freely. I think they understood that their father's relationship with me was making him happy again after the stress and pain of his divorce and was reducing some of the tension between him and their mother. Early in our relationship, Jim told me how he had gone over to the house to help Ben wash the car for ex-wife Denise and that everyone got along and had a good time, but most of all how happy it had made the boys that their parents were getting along.

I went back up to Jim's at the end of December to spend my thirty-seventh birthday and the New Year with him. We were already talking about getting married, though we didn't make specific plans right away. Jim was the relationship that some people wait a whole lifetime for and never get. How can anyone describe the gift of love at first connection? I was even comfortable filling him in about the work the scientists were doing with me.

In November, I had received a letter from Dr. Parker letting me know that they were in the final stages of writing up their preliminary results and getting approval for the next step in their study of me. Jim was intrigued and supportive and not the least put off. To reach such a place of tranquillity and security and romance and magic at that point in my life was almost unfathomable. Suddenly I had the chance to become a wife and to start a family as I had always dreamed of doing. Though I wouldn't know

Jim for long, he gave me a new strength and perspective on life that has profoundly transformed me.

If not for Jim, I don't know how I would have gotten through the move from our house in Encino, which we had lived in for twenty-eight years. My father was retiring, and my parents wanted to move to a smaller place. That fall, they filled me in that they were going to be looking for a new house. In the past, the prospect of moving had thrown me into paroxysms of anxiety; I had begged and pleaded with them not to do it and forced them to stay in LA, becoming a wreck. Moving out of the house wasn't as bad as moving across the country, but the idea was still terribly upsetting to me, and Jim helped me accept the news without falling into one of my panics. I realized that for the first time in my life, I was ready to live with the memories of my past and, if not exactly leave them behind, accept that I could take them with me and move on.

In December 2002 Jim and I had a conversation that changed the course of everything. He was unhappy with his job and frustrated that we weren't together all the time, and one night when he was sharing those thoughts with me, I suddenly asked him, "If you could go anywhere, where would you go?" To my surprise, he shot right back with "Tennessee." It turned out that his company was opening up a plant there, and he thought moving there might be an opportunity for a fresh start. To my even greater surprise, I found myself responding, "Let's go." He said, "Okay," and that was that. I had a good deal of trepidation about the idea, but I also sensed that it was vital that I make the commitment. I felt that Jim had come along to save my life, and I was going to let him save it, no matter how anxiety provoking that might be along the way. Knowing that he and I were going to be starting off on a life adventure was, for a start, a great help to me in coping with packing all of my huge collection of mementos up and coming to terms with moving out.

I had always known there would be a day that my parents would sell our house and I would have to pack everything up, but as the years went on and we kept living there, I continued to keep things. Not only had I filled my own bedroom up with my stuff, I had taken over my brother's room in October 1991, and it was crammed full. I still had my things from New Jersey and New York on top of twenty-eight years of California accumulations. I had a lifetime of stuff to go through.

On Saturday, January 11, 2003, I started to pack. It took five weeks to organize, pack, and load a portable storage container that we ordered, which was the size of a small garage. If you've ever gone through a cache of keepsakes, cleaning out a desk drawer or an overstuffed closet, you've probably been plunged into your past—finding photos you'd lost track of, maybe college mementos or toys of your children that you had stowed away. Memories rush through your head, taking you back to people you hadn't thought about in years, or trips you'd taken, special times with long-lost friends, or time spent with loved ones who've passed on. Hours can go by, and it's like reliving your life. It can be emotionally exhausting. Packing up all of my artifacts was one of the most grueling and emotionally depleting experiences of my life, and I don't know if I could have done it if not for Jim having come into my life. For the first time, I was beginning to focus on the future instead of the past.

On Friday, January 17, Jim came down to Los Angeles for a four-day weekend. He and I had started to talk seriously by then about getting married and moving to Tennessee, and it was time for him to meet my extended family. It was my mother's birthday, and she used that as an excuse for everyone to come over and meet him. It had been two weeks since I had last seen him, and I was so happy when he walked into my office. When everyone heard he was there, they all came in, one by one, and before I could say anything, he was engaged in three different conversations. I spent the weekend introducing him to family and friends, and everyone loved him. We also mentioned our plans about moving to Tennessee to my parents, which they were much less pleased about. They were worried that we were being impetuous, and truth be told, so was I, but my worries about that weren't going to stop me.

For the next month, I was in the throes of packing. Into the storage unit went all of my stuffed animals; my Madame Alexander dolls and my Barbies; my library of over 250 books; my video library of almost a thousand tapes; my Internet research library, my record albums and 45s, and all the homemade tapes I had made for more than twenty years. The more I packed up and the closer the move came, the more my mind was assaulted with an overflow of memories and the more dread I began to feel. Thank God for Jim.

On Monday, February 17, 2003, I cried as the storage container was being forklifted onto the truck that would take it away. The driver asked, "Why the tears?" and I told him that I had never been separated from my stuff before. He had no idea just what a crazy, obsessive, meticulously organized, and memory-drenched payload he was hauling away. I took a picture of the unit before I locked it up, filled to the rim, and as I watched the truck drive off, I realized that for the first time, I had the strength to grapple with my memory's inability to accept change or leave anything behind. I felt ready to live with the unrelenting memories of my past while at the same time moving on. It was because I had Jim next to me that I was able to stand there and watch that truck drive away and didn't feel that my life was being ripped away from me. He had begun to change me in a deep and abiding way.

I had no idea what a short time, in the end, I would have with him, and I will always be grateful for the long days we spent together in the next months as we began to plan our new life.

CHAPTER TEN

The Memory as Memorial

He saw all these forms and faces in a thousand relationships become newly born. Each one was mortal, a passionate, painful example of all that is transitory. Yet none of them died, they only changed, were always reborn, continually had a new face: only time stood between one face and another.

—Hermann Hesse, *Siddhartha*

I've heard that one of the terrors that people feel when they lose a loved one is that they will forget the sound of that person's voice; that more and more memories of times together will fade away through the years and that the sparkle of her eyes or the touch of his hand will recede into the vague mists of hazy recollection. This is one way in which my memory has proven to be a comfort; I have never had to feel that fear about losing my memories of Jim. Our time together was much too short, but I know that I will not forget a moment of it.

Our house went up for sale on Tuesday, February 18, 2003, and that same day I sent out invitations for a party at the house on Saturday, March 1, 2003. I had told my mother that I wanted to have one last big get-together in the house before we moved, and she said that would be great. What she didn't know was that Jim and I were planning that this would be our wedding day.

When we had told my parents about our intentions to marry and move, they had suggested we wait, and I would have preferred to plan more myself. Acting on such impulse was totally out of character for me, as much as anything I've ever done, and I understood why my parents were worried. But I was determined that I was going to act; Jim wanted to marry me and move to Tennessee, and no matter how much I might have preferred to plan a wedding and to stay in LA, I was going to do this his way. I didn't want a lot of time to think about it, and I never second-guessed. I just did it. Though previously, any thought of change had terrified me, now I was finding it wonderfully exhilarating, if somewhat scary, to be taking this huge step forward, and I plunged myself into the prospect of a new life with him.

On Sunday, February 23, 2003, Jim moved down to Los Angeles to stay with us until he and I took off. My mother said she had never seen me smile with such pure joy as I did that day when he arrived at the house. I could see that she was beginning to understand how good he was for me, which was a relief, because the next day Jim and I told my parents that the party we were having on Saturday was actually going to be our wedding. I will never forget my mother's face when she realized I was giving her only five days to prepare.

We got married in my parents' living room on Saturday, March 1, 2003, in a lovely ceremony that is one of the times of my life that I am deeply grateful I will always remember with perfect clarity. We invited seventy-five people, and I was appreciative that Jim's ex-wife had agreed to let their boys come. The house was filled with candles, the pool lights glistened outside, and the night was so magical that I felt as if I was hovering above things—almost the way that people describe an out-of-body experience. I had waited my whole life to get married and there I was, so happy that I felt as if I was floating.

A week after our wedding, we took off on our adventure across the country, leaving early in the morning on Saturday, March 8. We stopped in Flagstaff, Albuquerque, Amarillo, and Little Rock before we arrived in Springfield, Tennessee, near the Kentucky border, at 3:00 on Tuesday afternoon, March 11, 2003. The next day we toured Springfield, checking in at a real estate agency and talking to the dean at a school where we thought we might enroll the boys. Our plan was that they would be joining us in September. That night, though, when Jim talked to the boys, we both knew as soon as he hung up that the move wasn't feeling right. The boys had told him how much they missed him, and Jim was torn up by the idea of going six months without them. He looked miserable when he went to sleep, and the next morning when he woke up, he turned to me, apologized, and said, "I can't do it. I'm too far away from them. Can we please go back?" To his great surprise, I was elated. I would have moved to Timbuktu with him if that was where he wanted to go, but I was hugely relieved that where he really wanted to be was back in California. We left Springfield at 1:00 P.M. on Thursday, March 13, forty-six hours after arriving, and we turned back into my driveway in Encino on Sunday, March 16, at 5:00 P.M.

We moved in with my parents to give us time to figure out a new long-term plan that we'd be truly happy with. Then our life together started to take a scary turn. Jim had been diagnosed when he was thirty-eight with type 1 diabetes, and that news had been hard for him to accept. In some kind of perverse denial, he hadn't been taking the medication that was prescribed to him, and now that neglect was starting to catch up with him. On Monday, April 7, when he got out of bed, he fell, and by the time we went to the doctor later that day, he had started to have a tingling feeling in his feet, a common symptom of type 1 diabetes caused by nerve damage. The doctor wrote him a prescription and told him he needed to start taking better care of himself.

Even as he was facing his own issues, Jim was a constant support for me as I confronted the fast-approaching
ordeal of our move out of the house. It was sold in mid-
April, and we were scheduled to move over the Fourth of
July weekend. My parents and Jim started to pack up the
house on Sunday, June 22, 2003, and I was told to start
packing the remainder of my things at that point. Even
with as much as I had moved out into the storage container, I still had piles of things packed away in my bedroom. I kept saying that it would be taken care of by the
time the movers arrived. But every time I tried to pack
something, I'd wind up emotionally distraught, with
memories coursing through my mind. Days went by, and
then late on the Fourth of July, I finally committed myself to tackling it. I told Jim he'd have to sleep in the other
room, because I'd be packing all night. But I was inca-
pacitated. At 6:00 A.M., I woke Jim up and told him I
needed his help. As I lay in bed in tears, he packed the
whole room up.

Even then, though, there was one last thing not
packed: a strip of wallpaper on which I had been writing
notes about my life since 1977. The wallpaper notations
started when I was eleven years old—on January 19,
1977, to be exact. That first day, I had just signed my name
and the date. As time went on I added more notes, just a
little bit about the day, like "100 degrees outside" or
"Happy 30th Birthday," always with the date. Suddenly I
became a complete wreck about leaving this piece of

wallpaper, with twenty-six years of personal history written on it, behind, and I became determined that I was going to get it off the wall if it was the last thing I did. I had everyone trying to think of ways to get it off the wall, and ultimately I had to scrape it off with a razor. It took ninety minutes of sweat, and many tears, but I did it. It was in pieces, but it was off! Today it is wrapped carefully in a box in my keepsake trunk. The wall did not fare so well, and I hoped the new owners would forgive me.

By mid-July Jim and I were settled in my parents' new home, and we were both working. I had a job working on a television special, and he had taken a job as the mechanic for a car dealership where my friend's husband worked. Best of all, the boys were staying with us.

Then I had another exciting experience with the scientists. In June 2003, they had asked me if I would be willing to come down to UCI for a presentation of their initial findings to the university's medical community, known as Grand Rounds, which was scheduled for Wednesday, August 13. The date finally came, and I found myself feeling up and excited. The idea of being presented to a whole room full of doctors was anxiety provoking, but the scientific work was exciting to me, and as I drove to Irvine that day, I was determined to conquer my fears and do whatever they needed.

Grand Rounds was held in a large lecture hall on the first floor of one of the medical buildings, and I waited in the lobby outside the lecture hall while Dr. McGaugh and

Dr. Parker introduced to those in the room the work they had done with me. When Dr. Parker finally came and brought me into the lecture hall, I made myself focus entirely on Dr. McGaugh, who was sitting at a table in the front of the room with a big whiteboard on the wall behind him. He asked me to tell the story of how I had contacted him, why I e-mailed him, and to describe our first meeting. More than fifty doctors were sitting there, dead quiet, staring at me.

Dr. McGaugh asked me to do my diagrams on the whiteboard, and I drew the time line of history, from 1900 to the present, and also the circles that I see for years. He pointed out that it was of interest to him that the diagram of the way I see the time line would be considered backward for most people, as it is drawn from right to left. He also commented that it was unclear if or in what way these visuals might cause my ability to know the exact day of the week a date falls on.

After the presentation, the doctors came by to say how fascinating this was. Some of Dr. Parker's students stuck around and asked me a host of questions about what it's like to remember everything and what I meant when I said I just "see" the day I'm remembering. I could see that they found my recall abilities hard to fathom. It was at this point that I began to believe that perhaps my memory might actually lead to some kind of contribution, whether in explaining normal memory or perhaps solving some mystery about how to treat memory loss. As

Dr. Parker would put it to me some time later, some scientific work has the effect of opening up a window onto new terrain that is rich for study, and that, she said, was what my case would be doing.

Doing Grand Rounds was like someone showing me a different vision of myself, one of a person with a rare condition that might be able to help people someday, and that was another turning point for me in coping with my memory. My work with the scientists would take another significant break after this, but at least I was assured that they would be continuing their investigations, and I felt confident that they were going to find answers of some kind that would explain to me why my mind worked the way it did.

Jim had helped me to loosen my emotional grip on my past, and the scientists were now giving me hope that somehow some good might come out of the bizarre phenomenon I'd been living with inside my head. I wasn't feeling so alone with the swirling of my memories anymore, and I felt that I was now on the path toward breaking free from my fear of the future and my obsession with the past. With Jim, I was finally beginning to live the life I had envisioned for myself when I was a small child.

Jim and I knew we wanted a family, and we were delighted when I became pregnant in September 2003. A few weeks later, to our great disappointment, I had a miscarriage. That was quite a blow—to learn all at once that I'd finally been starting on the family I'd always wanted, but that it wasn't going to work out this time. But Jim insisted that we would keep trying, and he promised me that before long, I'd be pregnant again. For Thanksgiving 2003 Jim and I went up to Napa, and I met his parents and the rest of his family. They were a big group, and suddenly, I had two brothers, one sister, and two sisters-in-law, twenty-two nieces and nephews, and one great-niece.

In the new year, Jim and I enjoyed a wonderful stretch of months, spending lots of time together and beginning to focus on longer-term plans. The boys came again for a month in the summer. My parents and Jim had become very close, and my brother, Michael, had fallen in love with him too. I was finally truly looking forward to my future.

Then in August 2004, Jim began feeling strange in a way that he found hard to describe; he couldn't pinpoint what the sensation was like, but he wasn't feeling right. My mother was concerned that it was his diabetes, and she regularly urged him to get himself checked out, but he was stubborn and he had a psychological block about the diabetes. He didn't seem to want to believe it was really a problem. On September 1, he was working outside in 108 degree heat and became extremely dehydrated. By the time he got home that night, he was feeling horrible, and the next day he stayed home. On Friday, September 3, 2004, we woke up and he said to me, "I don't want to scare you, but my whole left side is numb."

Terrified, I called 911, and we were at the hospital all

day. They took test after test but could not find anything wrong, and without giving him a clear diagnosis, they finally sent him home. He began to feel a little better on Saturday and Sunday of Labor Day weekend, though when my parents had a party that Monday, Jim didn't come out of our room the entire day. He told me he thought he'd be well enough to go back to work on Tuesday, but that morning, I couldn't wake him up, and I was so unnerved that I went to get my mom and together we shook him. Finally he opened his eyes, and he stared at me with a look of such fright that it terrified me. I thought he might be in diabetic shock, and this time I couldn't even wait for an ambulance. We took him to the hospital ourselves. The doctors ran tests on him and he stayed overnight, and the next day he was told that his diabetes was the problem and that he had to start taking it much more seriously.

The reality that the disease was catching up with him seemed to have hit him very hard, and that Friday, he quit his job and took off for Napa. He hadn't said a word to me that he was leaving, but I did discover that he'd left me a letter in our mailbox. I went into a kind of emotional shock as I read it; just like that, our marriage was over. For the next three days, I was almost catatonic, holed up at home clutching his letter in disbelief. Even his ex-wife called me to say how shocked she was. Then at 6:00 P.M. on Tuesday, September 14, Jim called. As soon as I heard his voice I started to cry. I told him that if he wanted to stay up in Napa, I would move up there and that I didn't care about anything but being with him. To my enormous relief, he answered that I didn't need to do that because he was coming back to LA. He came home a week later. As he sat on our bed with tears rolling down his cheeks trying to explain, I just kissed him on his face and that was that. He was back. It was done. We never spoke of it again. I wish I could say that was the end of the drama in our lives, but fate had more in store for us.

On my thirty-ninth birthday in late December, Jim and I had dinner with my parents, and while my mother was making a toast, I suddenly got a horrible feeling that someone sitting at the table would not be here on my fortieth birthday. That was the beginning of a long period of dread that gripped me, which no matter what I tried over the next several months, I couldn't shake. I began to make special note of how suddenly some people were confronted with the harsh reality of death. On January 10 a mudslide in La Conchita, just north of LA, killed ten people in their homes. The news reported about one man who had gone out for ice cream right before and had lost his whole family. The suddenness of the tragedy unnerved me, and I started to feel more and more on edge. On January 21, I was out with Jim and our friend Andi, and I finally tried to verbalize how I was feeling, telling them that I felt as if I was hanging from the top of a cliff upside down by my toes. Then on Wednesday, January 26 at 6:03 A.M., a man left his Jeep on the Metro link train tracks, and eleven passengers on the train were killed when it barreled into the car. Jim woke me up to tell me about it, and I remember looking at him and thinking how horrifying it was that people could say good-bye in the morning to their loved ones, thinking they would see them that night and then never see them alive again.

Jim was working on thinking about more pleasant things. In early January 2005 he saw a job listed in the newspaper for a forklift repairman in the town of Santa Maria, two hours north in central California. He told me he wanted to apply for it and move us up there, and though that was farm country and I'd never relished a rural life I was resolved that if that's what would make Jim happy, that's what we'd do. We planned that once we got settled in up there, we'd start our family. He got the job, starting a spell of a long two-hour commute up to work and back every day. Our new life was getting under way, but even though he had focused my attention on our future, I still couldn't shake the sense of dread I was feeling.

On March 15 Jim and I were in a Chinese restaurant, and when I opened my fortune cookie, there was no fortune in it. I'm superstitious, and with all of the foreboding I'd been feeling, that was more than a little unsettling to me. He could see the look on my face, so he asked for a couple more, and when I opened another one, again there was no fortune. Jim's fortune said, *Your life will change forever,* and though with our plans for moving up to Santa

Maria in the works that should probably have been a good omen, it only seemed ominous to me. I started to become convinced that I was going to die.

Death seemed to be calling out for attention. On March 20, I found out that one of my best friends from junior high school had died of cancer in late February. She would have been forty years old on March 22. This was also the week that Terri Schiavo was taken off life support, and Jim and I had a conversation about what we'd want the other to do if we were in her situation. He told me he'd want me to pull the plug, but I told him not so for me; he'd have to carry my dead body around with him, because I was never going to leave him.

Wednesday, March 23, Jim and I had a wonderful dinner with my parents. I had received some questions by e-mail from Dr. Parker that day for a paper the scientists were working on about my case. The questions were actually for my mom, and so after dinner, we all sat around and answered them. I was heartened that they were moving forward with a paper about my case, and I couldn't wait to read more fully about their findings. That was a wonderful, warm family night, and as it turned out, it was the last such night we would ever share with Jim.

The next night as I got on the computer to e-mail my mom's responses to Dr. Parker, Jim told me he wasn't feeling well and was going to bed early. As I wrote my e-mail to Dr. Parker, I thought to myself that maybe I should get off the computer and spend some time with

Jim. A little while later, though, he came in to give me a kiss goodnight.

The next morning, March 25, Good Friday, we were up and out of bed by 4:00 A.M. as usual. I made his lunch while he got ready for work, and then we sat and talked while he ate his breakfast. At 5:00 A.M. I hugged and kissed him good-bye, and I listened as he drove away into the darkness. I will always be haunted by the vision of Jim walking out the door that morning into the darkness, and as poignant as that memory is, and as hard as it is for me to go back and back to, the vividness with which I will retain that memory for the rest of my life is also a great gift. Because he had a two-hour drive to work, he always called me along the way. That morning he called at 6:00 and again at 7:30, and the last thing he ever heard me say to him was that I loved him.

At 9:38, I was on the computer, responding to a message from Dr. Parker acknowledging mine of the night before. The subject line of her message was "the future," and she had asked me whether I knew days of the week for dates in the future in the same way I knew them for dates in the past. Could I, for example, say what day of the week September 25, 2005, would be, or January 8, 2007? I answered that I could see the days of the week through the end of 2005, but after that, the future was blank. I added, though, that in regard to the future, I had been thinking a good deal about it lately, because I was about to turn forty and I "would like to step into the next part of my life with a clean slate." Those e-mails back and forth seem eerie to me now, given what happened the very next moment.

At 9:40, just as I sent my e-mail, my cell phone rang. It was my mother telling me that she wanted to talk to my father. *Why hadn't she called him then?* I wondered. She hadn't wanted me to get the news over the phone. Her number at work was Jim's second emergency contact number, and his boss had called her because he couldn't reach me at home. Our Internet connection went through our landline, so the phone line had been busy. After talking to my mother, my dad came in and told me that Jim had collapsed at work and had been rushed to the hospital. At first I couldn't even understand what my father was saying. When I called the hospital moments later, they told me that he was unconscious, and my mind went into shock. The rest of that conversation is a blank in my mind; the next thing I remember is hearing the theme music to *The Price Is Right* on TV after I'd hung up the phone.

My mother came and picked me up, and we drove the two hours north. I spoke to the emergency room nurse three times during the trip, but there was no change. When we arrived, we were rushed into the emergency room to see him. My forty-two-year-old husband was lying in a coma on life support. A vision that will haunt me for the rest of my life is that when we walked into his room, his eyes were open, looking dead, like a doll's eyes. So began six days of hell.

Jim was moved to the critical care unit, and I stayed by his side all day and most of the night for all those days. My mom stayed in a motel with me, and my brother and my dad drove up regularly. Jim's mom came, along with his sister and brothers. Our family friend Beverly arrived, and my friend Wendy came to give support. We sat vigil, we comforted one another, and we prayed.

The doctors ran a battery of tests to try to determine what had happened to Jim, and on Saturday morning they informed us that he had suffered a massive stroke; a blood clot had exploded in his brain stem, almost surely the result of his diabetes. The nurses told me that he might be able to hear me, so I bought a bundle of magazines and read to him. In *People* there was a review of the movie *Guess Who,* a remake of *Guess Who's Coming to Dinner,* which I loved, and I suddenly found myself singing the theme song of that movie, "The Glory of Love." Up to that point Jim had not made a single movement in all the time I had sat with him, but as I started in on the song for a third time, suddenly his body jerked violently from side to side. I was sure that he was trying to tell me to stop singing, and I didn't know whether to laugh or cry. I clung desperately to that sign that he had heard me—that he was still alive in there and would make it through this.

On Monday, the third day that Jim had been in a coma, his doctor came in and started talking to me about organ donation. I was stunned. I was still praying desperately that he would miraculously snap back to life as people in comas sometimes do, and I wasn't ready for that discussion yet. Then, at 3:00 P.M. on Wednesday, the doctors attending Jim called a family meeting and informed us that the results of a CAT scan had shown that he had almost no brain activity. They were going to be declaring him dead at 5:30. I felt as if my insides were being ripped out of me, and I put my head down on the table and let out a horrifying sound that sends a shock through me every time I relive those moments again in my mind.

I've heard that in times like that, confronted with such devastating news, a person often goes into automatic, operating on some sort of emergency backup system in the mind, and I believe that's what happened to me. Jim's mother and I talked with the doctors about the organ donation procedure at 5:00 P.M. that day, and then I signed the consent papers. It wouldn't be until the next day that they harvested the organs. I had decided that there was one part of Jim that I was determined to keep. We had planned to start a family, and now those dreams of doing so together were shattered, but I asked the doctors if they would harvest his sperm, in the hope that I would someday be able to have his baby. At first, they refused, and I couldn't get them to budge, but then my dad went to the hospital administrators and told them a moving story.

When we had gone to pick up the car Jim had driven to work that last morning, we had discovered the lunchbox that I had packed for him still sitting on the backseat. My dad had taken it back to our house in LA, and as he cleaned it out, he saw that the food had started to spoil, and his eyes had filled with tears. My family had embraced Jim and come to love him, and it was at that moment that the truth sank in to my dad that Jim would never be coming back. He said to the hospital administrators that as they knew, Jim's body would spoil as surely as that lunch had spoiled, but that harvesting his sperm was a way for me to preserve at least some part of him and possibly create some happiness out of a horrible tragedy. After a good deal of deliberation, the hospital consented.

For hours on the morning before the organ donation procedure, before the surgical team came and took him off support, I sat holding Jim's hand. Even legally dead, he wasn't going without a fight. When the nurses walked in to begin preparing for the procedure, his heart raced wildly, and one of the nurses said to me that he was stubborn. She was right about that. He was strong and stubborn, and I believe he had hung on with all of his might. I gave Jim one last kiss and without looking back, I walked out of the room.

My mom cut a lock of his hair and put it in a box given to us by the organ donation network, and I have kept that box next to my bed ever since. I put his glasses inside, and his wallet, and several other mementos.

Since Jim's death I've felt that he is watching over me, giving me strength to live the way that he would have helped me to if we had been given more time together. I like to say that he's been sprinkling me with fairy dust. In those first few days after his passing, I was to perceive a number of signs of his presence. The night before his funeral, I was feeling horribly depressed, waiting at home for Jim's mom to show up; she was going to be staying with us. The new house we'd moved to was on a quiet street, and all of a sudden outside in front of our house, half a dozen police cars came screeching to a halt, with lights flashing and sirens blaring. They had surrounded a civilian car, which I learned later they had been chasing through the streets. I couldn't believe it—this major incident happening on our quiet street. Then, though I know it sounds crazy, the thought occurred to me that knowing how I loved car chases, Jim had sent this excitement to me to lift my spirits.

Another sign, I felt, was that my bereavement ribbon kept falling off. In the Jewish religion, mourners wear a black ribbon that is ripped by hand or cut with a razor blade in symbolism of the times when people tore their clothing as an expression of grief for their loss. We were all wearing them, but mine was the only one that kept falling off. Everywhere I turned, it was on the floor. Then I realized Jim didn't want me to walk around with that ribbon, a mark of my widowhood, and the next day it continued to fall off. I would pin it on again, and then find it later on the living room floor or in the kitchen. Finally, on Monday, April 4, when I met my friend Andi for dinner, the ribbon blew away in the wind when I got out of my car. I felt that was a message from him telling me he wanted me to go on with my life.

The eeriest sign came from one of the people who had received his organs. After they had all been operated on, I was told a little about them and given word about how they had fared. Jim's right kidney was transplanted into a sixty-five-year-old man who was married and had four children. He was a hotel owner but was disabled due to his illness. After his receipt of the kidney, he was doing well. The liver recipient was a forty-five-year-old married man who enjoyed reading, watching old movies, and doing Native American beadwork. He had been on the waiting list for almost three years. Following the transplant, his liver function was good, and he was recovering at home with his wife. The heart recipient was a sixty-eight-year-old married man with two children who worked as a dentist and enjoyed cooking for his family. Prior to the transplant, he had suffered from cardiomyopathy, a disease of the heart muscle that is often fatal. He had received the heart successfully, and it was functioning well. The last was a thirty-year-old woman, who received Jim's left kidney. She was single and lived with her family and had been on the waiting list for five years. She was "doing superb" according to the transplant coordinator, and her kidney function was great.

The organ donation network had told me that I would not be able to meet the people who were receiving Jim's

232

organs, and that most likely they would not contact me, but the coordinator I spoke to suggested that I might want to write a letter about Jim and our life together, which would be put on file in case any of his recipients ever wanted to know about him. I did so, and miraculously, I got a call that I had received a letter from the recipient of Jim's left kidney. She expressed her gratitude, telling me she felt the donation was a blessing from God, and then she wrote something that startled me. After she'd returned home from the surgery, every morning she felt she had to have a grilled cheese sandwich. "I don't know if that was one of your husband's favorite things," she wrote, "but I craved one all the time." I couldn't believe it. Jim loved grilled cheese sandwiches.

She ended her letter by saying that if I would like to contact her, she would love to hear from me, and February 2006, I met the woman I now affectionately refer to face-to-face as "left kidney." It was the Monday of Washington's Birthday, eleven months after Jim died. My mom came with me. When the recipient and her mother and the coordinators came in, she just grabbed me and hugged me, and as I put my hand on her back, I remember feeling that it was Jim in there. She gave me roses, and we sat down and talked. Meanwhile my mom started talking to her mother, and brought up the sudden craving for grilled cheese sandwiches. Her mother laughed, "Grilled cheese sandwiches nothing. This is a girl who didn't like dairy; now she needs to drink a gallon of milk a day." My mom and I just stared at one another in disbelief. Jim absolutely loved milk; he drank it with every meal; he drank it by the gallons. They also drank the same kind of milk: 2 percent.

Before Jim passed away, I would have expected that I would have simply stopped living if he had died; I would have thought I would crawl up into a catatonic ball and drive myself mad with remembering him. In the face of Jim's death, the Jill of a few years earlier would have collapsed in a mental hell of racing memories, refusing even to admit I would need to let him go. But Jim had changed me. I was devastated by losing him, but I found that I was determined in the face of this crisis to deal with it the way Jim would have wanted me to. This was the most profound experience I had ever gone through, and the reality and finality of death shook me to the core. I realized in a deep way that I had no choice but to accept the horrible twist of fate we had been dealt and to go on.

I dreaded the first morning after I buried him—waking up a widow—and I stayed in bed most of the day. Finally, at 6:00 P.M. I reluctantly forced myself out of bed to meet Andi for dinner. I know that it was only because Jim would have been disappointed in me if I hadn't gone on with my life that I was able to do so. Then next morning, I got out of bed and sat in a chair; that was the best I could do.

The next several months were a struggle. I could not stop thinking about Jim, flashing back to all of our times together, reliving and reliving those six days in the hospital. I walked around in a haze and cried almost continuously, spending many days largely in solitude, cycling through memory after memory of him. When my parents went out, I would call them continually, worried that something might have happened to them. I was shell-shocked by the memory of the call about Jim having collapsed, and I couldn't shake the fear I might get another call like that at any moment. To this day, I do not go anywhere without my cell phone so that I can check in with my family regularly to make sure they are okay. I found that I couldn't drive down certain streets because they would remind me too vividly of a particular day with Jim, and I still can't drive down them. I had to sell his car before long because it was too painful to see it sitting there in our driveway.

During the grieving process, many people spend a great deal of time absorbing themselves in memories of their loved one and turn inward. In what's called traumatic grief, people become intensely fixated on persistent memories of their loved one, searching desperately for the lost presence of that person, and they often are thrown into a chaotic state of mixed emotions: anger, despair, envy of those who have not suffered the same loss, and often a paralyzing sense of life's futility. I felt all of those things, and at times couldn't conceive of going on, but then I'd feel Jim's presence again and know that he was urging me to embrace life.

Due to that feeling that he was watching over me, I forced myself to function at least on a basic level. I thought back to the breakdown I had when my mother was ill, and I was determined that I wasn't going to let myself break down again. Jim had emboldened me with a new determination to live my life the way that he would have lived his. This time I would not collapse. This time I would get back on my feet. I felt his presence, and I knew that was what he wanted.

His death made me realize how short life is and how suddenly things can change, no matter how desperately we try to stop the process. I was about to turn forty, and I realized I didn't have the time to lose. I just decided, for the first time, I was going to take the punch and accept the fate that had been dealt me. I began to see in a new, deeper way that my memory had kept me much too chained to my ever-insistent past and that I had not been able to focus at all enough on the future. I had finally begun to do so with Jim, and I was determined to keep forging forward.

I've found no escape from the repetition in my mind of the day Jim collapsed, or the call from his work, or the six days I sat by his hospital bed. I find myself remembering those moments every day, and I fully expect that I will continue to do so every day for the rest of my life. I had always been afraid of death, and then after only twenty-nine months of the one true love I had ever known, my husband walked out the door one morning and died. Though remembering those last days of Jim's life is horribly painful, in this regard, my memory has been a double-edged sword. I also have the comfort of knowing that I will remember everything about him vividly and all of the wonderful days I spent with him, for the rest of my life.

In the grieving process, though memories of the loved one can be intensely painful, it seems that remembering is a more powerful salve than repressing or avoiding thoughts about the loved one. A specialist on grieving, Dr. Mardi Horowitz, has found that "at a wake or memorial service, those who were least battered by the death will have the most memories of the deceased." And after the initial phase of shock and denial about a loved one's death, reminiscing about times spent together is important in helping the healing process move forward and in building a new relationship with the loved one, which can be thought of as the memory relationship. What a wonderful concept.

Many widows report a continuing sense of their deceased husbands' presence and find a good deal of comfort from that. A good number of widows experience what are reported as hallucinations of their husbands— actually hearing him or feeling they've been touched by him, and calling up memories of such instances of feeling his presence may help a good deal in coping with the loss. Most often, these sensations of continuing physical presence fade after about two years, but one fascinating aspect of the grieving process many widows go through is that the sense of the continued presence of their husbands is eventually internalized, so that they feel their deceased partner is living within them as an enduring companion. That is exactly how I feel about Jim.

In addition to the salve of reminiscing, a powerful source of understanding and strength in coming to terms with the loss of a loved one is talking with others who have suffered the same fate. I was extremely fortunate in the months after Jim passed away to join a bereavement group for widows, which has become a deeply cherished circle of friends. The first day I showed up to join the group, I walked into the room and marveled that one of the women was laughing about something; the thought of laughing, about anything, was beyond comprehension to me at the time. The entire room gasped when they saw me because I was so young. They were all twenty to forty years older than me; one woman, Marj, had been married for almost sixty years; another, Arlene, who was seventy-five, told me that she'd been married when she was sixteen. I wondered what I was doing there. What would these women from other generations and I have to say to one another?

We ended up having a great deal to say, and we are still talking. I get together with them now every Thursday night for dinner, whatever else may be going on in our lives. These caring and thoughtful ladies have been invaluable in helping me to reengage with life. If these women who had lost companions with whom they'd spent more years than I had even been alive could accept their losses and face their futures, then so could I. They've treated me almost as their collective child, and if I do ever have the baby that Jim and I dreamed of, he or she will have the great good fortune to have eight lovely, fawning grandmothers.

The day that Jim suffered his stroke, I had written to Dr. Parker that I was looking forward to my fortieth birthday and moving into a new phase of life with a clean slate. I would never have believed when I wrote those words that I would be moving into that new life without Jim or that I would have been capable of doing so. The ladies have helped me to understand that in losing those we love, it isn't moving on that we want to do, in truth; we want to carry them with us, to keep them inside us and hold them close, hearing them speak to us just as they did, feeling their presence, looking into their eyes and knowing that they are with us always. This, I know with complete certainty, I will be able to do with Jim, and after a lifetime of struggle, my memory has proven at last in this one special way to be a source of abiding solace.

I have learned a great deal through the course of working on this book about the ways in which memory shapes our lives. The more I have learned, the more amazing I have found the remarkable feats of memory to be. Surely, of all the many ways in which memory enriches our lives, this ability it bestows on us to hold fast to our lost loved ones is one of its most precious gifts.

EPILOGUE

In July 2005, I got a call from Dr. Parker informing me that the scientific paper that she, Dr. McGaugh, and Dr. Cahill had been working on about their study of me was ready for me to read. They were going to submit it to a scientific journal, and they wanted me to tell them about anything they'd written that I thought was inaccurate in describing how my memory works or too personal for publication. Their findings were judged to be strong, and the paper, with the title "A Case of Unusual Autobiographical Remembering," was eventually published in a prestigious journal of brain science, *Neurocase*, in February 2006.

Dr. Parker had written to me earlier to give me a summary of what they'd determined, but reading the full paper was nonetheless quite an experience. They referred to me as "AJ" in order to preserve my anonymity, but the person I was reading about was most certainly Jill; they had captured so much so beautifully about the experience of my life. Their opening line told me that they had understood, deeply, how hard living with my memory had been for me: "What would it be like to live with a memory so powerful that it dominates one's waking life?"

As Dr. Parker had explained to me, they had decided to take an approach to studying me that would let me fully tell my story, to which they would listen carefully, and then they would seek to verify, through their testing, the things I had reported to them. As I continued to read their paper, I began to cry, because I felt they had captured so accurately all I had told them, and had verified it all in such vivid detail, and I felt truly understood for the first time in my life.

In fifteen tightly crafted pages, they had summarized all the results of their many tests of me. They reported how accurately I had responded on all their tests about dates and events, describing my answers to the Easter tests, and to the test of dates and events that Dr. McGaugh had given me the first day I met him, as well as to their spontaneous quizzes on the many other occasions. They also described in detail the results of the neurological testing. Reading an actual scientific paper about the findings was somewhat disconcerting, but doing so also conveyed to me in a new and deeper way that the characteristics of my memory functioning have to do with the way my brain operates. They are not simply matters of my perception; they are scientifically proven facts.

My general memory index—a concept somewhat related to that of general intelligence, in that it is a conglomerate measure of a range of memory abilities—was very high, near the ceiling; and I got perfect scores on nine of the tests that measured more specific memory functions. As I wrote before, the scientists explained that they do not know how much higher I might have scored on those tests if they had been designed to measure even higher ability. The skills that I was especially high on included visual memory; interpreting people's facial expressions, called "face perception"; smell identification; and sensory perception, which was strong support for my self-reports about the intensity of my sensory memory. I did relatively poorly on four of the tests, which measured such things as my ability to recall a list of words and a test of memory for faces, which is memorization of a particular face rather than "reading" a person's face. Those results provided strong support, as Dr. Parker had indicated to me earlier, for my reports about having such trouble memorizing. In addition, I scored in the average range for a whole set of tests of various cognitive abilities, such as semantic memory, which is the knowledge of basic facts that we've learned; and verbal memory for things recited to me that I had to recite back.

The particular strengths and weaknesses revealed by the neurological tests, in combination with the other data the scientists had from testing me, and from my own descriptions of how automatic my memory is, led them to posit that there may well be structural features of my brain that prevent me from turning off what is called episodic retrieval, the recall of events from our lives. Brain scanning has revealed that particular areas of the right and left cerebral cortex—the large "thinking center" of the human brain—are involved with retrieval of episodic memory, and the scientists pointed to the possibility that my brain may have some anomalies in those areas. As they wrote, "AJ seems unable to turn off episodic retrieval mode as in normal individuals." They also indicated that my memory did, therefore, open up significant new terrain for research. They wrote: "There has been research on brain regions involved with episodic retrieval mode, but not on superabundant autobiographical memory as it has not been identified before." In keeping with just how complex and mysterious a function memory is, though, they also wrote that there may be no direct link between what the neurological tests showed about my cognitive abilities and the way my memory works. Further work will have to address that question.

The results of the testing led the scientists to conduct brain scanning on me in August 2006. They used the MRI technique, in which magnetic and radio waves make a highly detailed image of the structure of the brain. Those scans were then sent to two specialists in the analysis of brain scans, Dr. Jill Goldstein at Harvard Medical School and Dr. Nikos Makris at the Neuroscience Center of Massachusetts General Hospital. The hope was that they would find anomalies in some areas of my brain that would lead to further pinpointing of what may be the structural reasons for the way my memory works. Just recently, I got the word that they had. Not only did they identify more than two dozen areas that are a good deal larger than normal, but some of them are extraordinarily large. As Dr. Cahill said, they are so large that it's "like the difference in size between Shaquille O'Neal and the rest of us." Doctors Goldstein and Makris have told me that they would like to continue studying my brain, and I am excited about the prospect of ongoing work with them.

My great hope now is that they will find clues in their further studies that will lead them down fruitful paths for treating or preventing memory loss. Dr. Cahill explained that a great deal of work is going on in the effort to identify the specific structures of the brain that account for particular cognitive functions, and that great headway has been made. He even said that, in experiments done with rats, "we make stronger memories. Maybe someday it will be possible to be able to do so in humans." I would be enormously gratified if the study of my memory and brain could in any way contribute to knowledge about how to do so.

I have gained enormous respect for the scientific process through the course of this adventure. Another thing Dr. Cahill said to me speaks powerfully about what a challenging yet thrilling process it is: "I like to describe science as this," he said. "You're at the edge of what we know and you're trying to push back that edge and so you're sticking your hands into the dark and you get bitten sometimes, but the cool thing about being a scientist is, ultimately, with enough persistence and luck, you touch something new. We push back the frontier of ignorance." What a beautiful enterprise, and one that I will gladly contribute as much of my time and self to as may seem to be valuable.

When the people in my life learn about my memory, they often ask me, Is having all those memories worth it? If you had your life to live again, would you want your memory to be the way it is, or would you give it up? The answer is that, despite all the pain it has caused me, if I could choose, I would keep my memory, because it's made me who I am. Though on balance I would say my memory has been more of a curse than a blessing, I think perhaps, with the scientific work progressing, some wonderful blessings are yet to come. The greatest of these would be if, even in some small way, the study of my memory were able to help someone.

So, in the end, my conclusion is hope. Rather than to be trapped by overriding compulsions, or by the awareness of every bad decision I have ever made and its consequences, or to be both tormented and comforted by the memories of my beloved husband and the impact of his sudden death, I intend to use the strength and learning I have gained to work toward the day when I am no longer the prisoner of my memory, but rather I am its warden.

GLOSSARY

Autobiographical memory: A person's memory of the specific events of his or her life as well as for general autobiographical facts, such as where one was born or that one is married.

Biases: Memory errors in which one's recollection is distorted by present attitudes or information, which break down into five types:

—Consistency bias causes us to make our thoughts and feelings more consistent over time

—Change bias occurs when we think something should have changed and our memory of the way things were earlier is distorted to cause us to perceive change

—Hindsight bias occurs when we think we always knew something that in fact we only just found out

—Stereotypical bias involves attributing qualities perceived to be true of a group onto an individual

—Egocentric bias involves remembering the past in ways that are self-aggrandizing and make ourselves more the center of events than we really were

Glossary

Childhood amnesia: The universal human forgetting of almost all of our memories from the first few years of our lives; studies show that long-term autobiographical memory begins at about age four.

Episodic memory: The memory of specific episodes in one's life; part of long-term, declarative memory. We construct our recollections of the events in our lives from retrieving these episodic memories.

Flashbulb memory: A memory that is extremely vivid, recalled with an almost photographic degree of detail; most often formed during a major life event of a dramatic or traumatic nature, or a shocking world event, such as when people remember what they were doing when the *Challenger* space shuttle exploded.

Hyperthymestic syndrome: The name given to autobiographical memory syndrome, the defining features of which are that the person spends an abnormally large amount of time remembering his or her personal past and also has an extraordinary capacity to recall specific events from his or her personal past. The co-occurrence of both defining features must be present. The name is derived from the Greek word *thymesis,* which means "remembering," and *hyper,* meaning "more than normal."

Memory bump: The well-documented increase in recall of autobiographical memories between the ages of approximately ten to thirty; we have many fewer memories from the years both before and after.

Memory inhibition: The process whereby many memories are inhibited from being stored in long-term memory for future retrieval. One theory argues that this is due to interference from new information coming into our brains. The process is thought to be important in culling out unnecessary or distracting memories.

Glossary

Method of loci: A system for memorizing of ancient origin, written about in the Latin text *Rhetorica ad Herennium,* dated to approximately 85 B.C. Using the method, one envisions a familiar location of some kind, such as a building, and associates pieces of information to be memorized with specific places within that location, as for example parts of a speech being associated with different rooms in a building. When seeking to remember the information, the person "travels" through these locations and the information is more easily recalled.

Misattribution: A form of incorrect remembering whereby we attribute a memory to the wrong source, such as when an eyewitness mistakes one person's face for another's or when we think we heard about something on TV when in fact a friend told us.

Motivated forgetting: The process whereby one intentionally pushes memories out of mind; sometimes referred to as purposeful forgetting; studies have shown that the practice is effective in limiting one's recall of those memories over time.

Narrative psychology: A branch of psychology concerned with how we make meaning out of the experiences of our lives by crafting stories and also by learning stories and listening to others' stories, in other words, the study of the way that stories shape our lives and our sense of self.

Neurobiology: The study of how neurons are organized into circuitry in our brains and how these circuits process information and affect our behavior.

Neuropsychology: The study of how the physical structures of the brain relate to psychological processes and symptoms; focuses on identifying areas of strength and of impairment, such as language disorders, cognitive impairments, and memory problems.

Personal event memories: A subtype of autobiographical memories that are particularly vivid, often highly emotional; usually, memories of dramatic or momentous events.

Repression: The concept put forward by Sigmund Freud that we force out of consciousness and recollection memories of events, usually ones that are traumatic or anxiety provoking.

Retrieval cue: A stimulus from the outside world, such as a sound or an image, that triggers our brain to retrieve a memory, such as when a song on the radio brings to mind a particular memory.

Self-defining memory: A memory to which one attributes particular importance and remembers especially clearly, and repeatedly, about a long-term issue or feature of one's life, which one feels helps to explain who he or she is as a person, usually provoking strong feelings.

Semantic memory: Our general knowledge of facts about the world, not necessarily specific to our own lives, such as the names of the capital cities of countries and that 1 plus 1 equals 2.

Suggestibility: The error in memory by which false memories are constructed from outside information, not information stored in our minds, such as notoriously in the case of false memories of child abuse that were created in children's minds.

Superior memory: Exceptionally strong memory, which may be in many different areas of memory performance, such as memory for long strings of numbers (as, for example, the digits of pi), or for written text. In most superior memory cases on record, no particularly strong recall for autobiographical events has been found.

Transience: The normal loss of memory for facts and events over time; considered a healthy clearing out of the mind to make way for more important information.

NOTES

CHAPTER ONE

Page 10   **On AJ's recall of dates and events:** Elizabeth S.
          Parker, Larry Cahill, and James L. McGaugh, "A Case
          of Unusual Autobiographical Remembering," *Neuro-
          case* 12 (2006): 35–49.

Page 19   **Background on Alexander Luria and cases S
          and VP:** John M. Wilding and Elizabeth R. Valentine,
          Superior Memory (New York: Psychology Press, 1997),
          pp. 22–29.

Page 23   **The Matrix of Numbers:** Exemplary matrix used
          by Alexander Luria to test his research subject S, as it
          appears in A. R. Luria, *The Mind of a Mnemonist: A Lit-
          tle Book About a Vast Memory* (1968; repr., Cambridge:
          Harvard University Press, 2006).

Page 30   **Drawings of historical time line and circles
          for months:** Parker et al., "A Case of Unusual
          Autobiographical Remembering."

Page 33   **Background on Endel Tulving's theory of retrieval cues:** "Endel Tulving: World Authority on Human Memory Function," www.Science.ca.

Page 34   **On involuntary memories, frequency of:** L. Kvavilashvili and G. Mandler. "Out of One's Mind: A Study of Involuntary Semantic Memories," *Cognitive Psychology* 48 (January 2004): 47–94.

Page 34   **On the preponderance of positive memories:** Dorthe Berntsen, "Involuntary Autobiographical Memories," in John W. Mace (Ed.), *Involuntary Memory* (Cambridge, Mass.: Blackwell Publishing, 2007).

Page 36   **On the absence of emotion in memories:** Denise R. Beike, "The Unnoticed Absence of Emotion in Autobiographical Memory," *Social and Personality Psychology Compass,* 1:1 (2007): 392–408.

Page 36   **On personal event memories:** David B. Pillemer, *Momentous Events, Vivid Memories* (Cambridge, Mass.: Harvard University Press, 1998).

CHAPTER TWO

Page 41   **Oliver Sacks:** "The Abyss," *New Yorker*, September 24, 2007.

Page 44   **On repression of memories:** Matthew Hugh Erdelyi, "The Unified Theory of Repression," *Behavioral and Brain Sciences* 29 (2006): 499–551.

Page 44   **On memory inhibition:** Michael C. Anderson, "Rethinking Interference Theory: Executive Control and the Mechanisms of Forgetting," *Journal of Memory and Language* 49 (2003): 415–445; Michael C. Anderson, *Active Forgetting* (New York: Haworth Press, 2001).

Page 47   **On pushing unwanted memories out of mind:** Benjamin J. Levy and Michael C. Anderson,

"Inhibitory Processes and the Control of Memory Retrieval," By *Trends in Cognitive Sciences* 6:7 (July 2002): 299–305.

Page 47　**On motivated forgetting in the long term:** Erdelyi, "The Unified Theory of Repression."

Page 48　**On Daniel Schacter's memory sins:** Daniel Schacter, *The Seven Sins of Memory* (Boston: Houghton Mifflin, 2001).

Page 51　**On the reconstruction of autobiographical memories:** "The Memory Experience: A Journey of Self Discovery," bbc.co.uk.

Page 56　**On ruminating and depression:** The work of Susan Nolen-Hoeksema is cited in Bridget Murray Law, "Probing the Depression-Rumination Cycle," *Monitor on Psychology*, www.apa.org.

Page 58　**On the trade-off of realism in optimism:** Martin Seligman Forum on Depression, Life Matters with Julie McCrossin, August 16, 2002, www.abc.net.

Page 58　**On 3 percent of events memorable:** Avril Thorne, "Personal Memory Telling and Personal Development," *Personality and Social Psychology Review*, 4:1 (2000): 45–56.

CHAPTER THREE

Page 62　**On recall of first memories:** The work of Avril Thorne is described in Carlin Flora, "Self-Portrait in a Skewed Mirror," *Psychology Today* (January–February 2006), 58–62, 64–65.

Page 63　**On memory capability at eighteen months:** Madeline J. Eacott, "Memory for the Events of Early Childhood," *Current Directions in Psychological Science* 8:2 (April 1999): 46–48.

Page 64 **On memory of reading before birth:** Mark L. Howe, "Review of The Fate of Early Memories," *American Journal of Psychiatry* 159 (June 2002): 1072–1073.

Page 64 **On infants' recognition of self:** Denise Beike et al., *The Self and Memory* (New York: Psychology Press, 2004) p. 48; Stanley B. Klein, Tim P. German, Leda Cosmides, and Rami Gabriel, "A Theory of Autobiographical Memory," *Social Cognition* 22:5 (2004): 460–490.

Page 64 **On age at which long-term memories begin:** Darryl Bruce, Angela Dolan, and Kimberly Phillips-Grant, "On the Transition from Childhood Amnesia to the Recall of Personal Memories," *Psychological Science* 11:5 (September 2000): 360–364.

Page 64 **Overview on theories of child amnesia:** Pirjo Korkiakangas, "Childhood Memories and the Conceptualization of Childhood," *Ethnologia Scandinavica* 24 (1994); Patricia J. Bauer, "Oh Where, Oh Where Have Those Early Memories Gone? A Developmental Perspective on Childhood Amnesia," Psychological Science Agenda, American Psychological Association, APA Online, www.apa.org.

Page 65 **On mind of infant so different from that of adult:** Henry Gleitman, Alan Fridlund, and Daniel Reisberg, *Psychology*, 6th ed. (New York: Norton, 2004), cited in entry on childhood amnesia, Wikipedia, en.wikipedia.org/wiki/Childhood amnesia.

Page 67 **On significance for memory of parents telling stories:** Avril Thorne, "Personal Memory Telling and Personality Development," *Personality and Social Psychology Review,* 4:1 (2000): 45–56.

Page 81 **On when children begin to forget:** Transcript of interview with Harlene Hayne, Science Show, ABC Radio National, June 3, 2006, www .abc.net.

CHAPTER FOUR

Page 100 **On the memory bump and memories vivid:** Dorthe Berntsen and David Rubin, "Emotionally Charged Autobiographical Memories Across the Life Span," *Psychology and Aging* 17:4 (2002): 636–652.

Page 101 **On explanations for the memory bump:** Johannes J. F. Schroots and Cor van Dijkum "Autobiographical Memory Bump: A Dynamic Lifespan Model," *Dynamical Psychology* (2004); Dennis Meredith, "Mining the Meaning of Memories," *Duke University Alumni Magazine* (March–April 1998), 84, no. 3, 14–18.

Page 102 **On later life memory bumps:** Monisha Pasupathi, "The Social Construction of the Personal Past and Its Implications for Adult Development," *Psychological Bulletin* 127:5 (2001): 651–672.

CHAPTER FIVE

Page 105 **Benedict Carey:** "This Is Your Life (and How to Tell It)," *New York Times,* May 22, 2007.

Page 106 **"Because the life story is . . .":** Pasupathi, "The Social Construction of the Personal Past."

Page 106 **"Our knowledge of self is very . . .** Stanley B. Klein, Tim P. German, Leda Cosmides, and Rami Gabriel, "A Theory of Autobiographical Memory," *Social Cognition* 22:5 (2004): 460–490.

Page 107 **On when children develop the ability to**

tell stories: T. Habermas and C. Paha, "The Development of Coherence in Adolescents' Life Narratives," *Narrative Inquiry* 11:1 (2001): 35–54.

Page 107 **Life story crafted starting in later adolescence:** Pasupathi, "The Social Construction of the Personal Past." Kate C. McLean et al., "Selves Creating Stories Creating Selves," *Personality and Social Psychology Review* 11:3 (2007): 262–278, Kate C. McLean and Michael W. Pratt, "Life's Little (and Big) Lessons," *Developmental Psychology* 42:4 (2006): 714–722.

Page 108 **Repeating stories at rate of 12 percent:** Flora, "Self-Portrait in a Skewed Mirror."

Page 109 **Negative memories crafted into life wisdom:** Susan Bluck and Judith Gluck, "Making Things Better and Learning a Lesson," *Journal of Personality* 72:3 (June 2004): 543–572.

Page 110 **Memory bump for positive events:** Berntsen and Rubin, "Emotionally Charged Autobiographical Memories"; David Rubin and Dorthe Berntsen, "Life Scripts Help to Maintain Autobiographical Memories of Highly Positive, But Not Highly Negative, Events," *Memory and Cognition* 31:1 (2003): 1–14; W. Richard Walker, John J. Skowronski, and Charles P. Thompson, "Life Is Pleasant—and Memory Helps to Keep It That Way!" *Review of General Psychology* 7:2 (2003): 203–218.

Page 122 **On lost selves:** Benedict Carey, "The New Year's Cocktail: Regret with a Dash of Bitters," *New York Times,* January 1, 2008.

CHAPTER SIX

Page 128   **"As one researcher who has worked . . .":** Thomas V. McGovern, "Seeking Socrates' Similes," PsychTeacher Electronic Discussion List, May 2005, http://teachpsych.org.

Page 128   **"Let's say I'm thinking . . .":** Dan McAdams quoted in Flora, "Self-Portrait in a Skewed Mirror."

Page 137   **On how life narratives change with circumstances:** Dan P. McAdams, *The Redemptive Self: Stories Americans Live* (New York: Oxford University Press, 2006); Dr. Bertram Cohler quoted in Daniel Goleman, "Personal Myths Bring Cohesion to the Chaos of Each Life," *New York Times*, May 24, 1988; Thorne, "Personal Memory Telling and Personality Development."

Page 137   **On Erikson's articulation of life's phases:** Leonie Sugarman, *Life-Span Development* (New York: Routledge, 1986).

Page 138   **McAdams's work on life narrative redemptive:** "Flora, Self-Portrait in a Skewed Mirror."

Page 143   **McAdams on life story as myth:** Daniel McAdams, *The Stories We Live By: Personal Myths and the Making of the Self* (New York: Morrow, 1993).

Page 143   **"New work by psychological researchers . . .":** Goleman, "Personal Myths Bring Cohesion to the Chaos of Each Life."

CHAPTER SEVEN

Page 146   **On the value of telling others our life stories and sharing memories within families:** Pasupathi, "The Social Construction of the Personal Past."

CHAPTER EIGHT

Page 186   **On Stroop test:** Stroop Task: A Test of Capacity to Direct Attention, www.snre.umich.edu.

Page 186   **On Proverbs Test:** Robert J. Sbordone, *Neuropsychology for Health Care Professionals and Attorneys* (Boca Raton, FL: CRC Press, 2000).

Page 190   **Table of Easter dates:** Parker et al., "A Case of Unusual Autobiographical Remembering."

CHAPTER TEN

Page 235   **On traumatic grief:** Shelby Jacobs, *Traumatic Grief: Diagnosis, Treatment and Prevention* (New York: Psychology Press, 1999); "Understanding the Grieving Process," www.About.com.

Page 237   **"At a wake or memorial service . . .":** Daniel Goleman, "Study of Normal Mourning Process Illuminates Grief Gone Awry," *New York Times*, March 29, 1988.

Page 237   **On widows feeling the presence of dead husbands:** Vijai P. Sharma, Ph.D., "One Year After Loss," www.mindpub.com.

EPILOGUE

Page 245   **"like the difference in size between Shaquille O'Neal . . .":** Amy Ellis Nutt, "Picturing the Past: How Science Is Mapping Memory," *Newark Star-Ledger*, December 10, 2007.

ACKNOWLEDGMENTS

I want to thank everyone who has worked with me on this book. I want them to know how much I appreciate all they have done. It hasn't been an easy road, nor have I been the easiest person to work with—but their kindness and dedication to me and my story will always be remembered. In that spirit, my sincere thanks to:

My writer, Bart Davis: The moment I heard his voice I knew he was the person to walk this journey with me. He understood from the beginning what my memory has done to my life. With his friendship and support, I have been able to tell my story.

My agent, Eileen Cope at Trident Media Group, whose professional guidance, understanding, and support were valuable beyond measure. She has stood by me every moment of the way.

Acknowledgments

Robert Gottlieb and Dan Harvey of Trident Media Group, whose belief and commitment were unflagging.

My editor, Emily Loose at Free Press, who moved from fascination to true understanding—and who to me is the standard for all editors. She has been truly devoted, spending countless hours in her quest for the best, most accurate, and meaningful story, and has made me proud to have my name on this book.

Free Press Publisher Martha Levin and Editorial Director Dominick Anfuso, whose enthusiasm could be felt from the beginning.

Free Press Publicity Director Carissa Hayes and my publicist Heidi Metcalfe, who have worked tirelessly to make sure my story reached the world.

Trident assistant Amy Meyerson and Free Press assistant Danielle Kaniper, who were always sweet to me even when maybe I wasn't.

My attorneys, Jonathan Erlich and Robert Strent, for their commitment to me and this project.

The girls in my bubble, with over a hundred years of friendship: Wendy Lavoie, Tina Roberts, Laura Green, Teri Levy, Andi Olden, and Caitlin Keats. Your love, understanding, and friendship have meant the world to me.

Those closest to me through the years: Bob Chafey, Jodi and Damian Greenberg, Gary Salem, Donna and Rob Bruza, Rochelle Hyman, Sara Escala, Vivienne Friedman, Melissa Buyer, Jan McGuire, Craig Lavoie, Barry Green, and Tres Pryor—I love you.

Acknowledgments

My stepsons, Ben and Tyler Price: I love you both and always will.

My aunt, Ruth Tillman, whom I felt most like and who always wanted the best for me.

Danny, Beverly, Matthew, and Adam Wells; Stuart, Deidre, Jennifer, Christopher, and Alexander Damon; Arnold, Carol, and Max Sank; Earl, Barbara, and Jennifer Kate Barret; and Miriam Garfield—with whom I spent my childhood. You are my second family, and I love you.

The women in my Bereavement Group: Cherie Beller, Phyllis Berke, Marj Bravin, Renee Gordon, Arlene Lottman, and Dalia Ulmer, for your wisdom, friendship, and total understanding.

My special thanks to the scientists at the University of California at Irvine, Dr. James L. McGaugh, Dr. Elizabeth S. Parker, and Dr. Larry Cahill, for listening to me and believing in me and for taking me on this incredible journey that has meant so much to my life. You showed me the way to understand myself and helped me to bring that understanding to others in the hope of advancing the science of human memory.

My new scientists, Dr. Jill M. Goldstein, Ph.D., and Dr. Nikos Makris M.D., Ph.D., with whom I will take the next part of my journey.

263